Leave Your Nets

Leave Your Nets

Joel S. Goldsmith

EDITED BY LORRAINE SINKLER

THE CITADEL PRESS   *Secaucus, N.J.*

Except the Lord build the house, they
labour in vain that build it.

—PSALM 127

Illumination dissolves all material ties and binds men together with the golden chains of spiritual understanding; it acknowledges only the leadership of the Christ; it has no ritual but the divine, impersonal, universal Love, no other worship than the inner Flame that is ever lit at the shrine of Spirit. This union is the free state of spiritual brotherhood. The only restraint is the discipline of Soul; therefore, we know liberty without license; we are a united universe without physical limits, a divine service to God without ceremony or creed. The illumined walk without fear —by Grace.

—The Infinite Way

Contents

———◂•▸———

Leave Your Nets

O N E

The Call

----------◄●►----------

God-consciousness is a plane of consciousness different from that experienced by "the natural man." The natural man is acquisitive, fearful, doubtful, and hesitant in thought and deed, all based on fears concerning the self. He lives in a sense of separation from God, but at some time in his experience, because of the depth and degree of his need, the natural man is turned inward to seek within himself for that which he outwardly requires. This inward turning becomes a search for God, a seeking for truth and, when earnestly and persistently followed, results in the dawning in consciousness of the Verities: the activities, laws, substance, and being of the Infinite Invisible. The natural man begins to "die," and the son of God is being raised up.

Now the seeker begins to realize some measure of his oneness with God, and he eventually discerns that Spirit really is the essence and very fiber of his being. The realization of divine sonship is unfolding, a conscious awareness of Spirit and Its law and being. The Christ, or son of God, is being born again in the manger of human consciousness, and evolves by stages to the degree of manhood in Christ, to the full stature of sonship or God-consciousness.

On this higher plane, the "old man" appears less and less. Now one becomes aware that this old man is not and never was a real entity, but rather that a false concept of the creative Principle and Its universe had been entertained and accepted as truth. More and more the awareness of true identity becomes manifest, and slowly truth dawns in consciousness, until God is beheld as one's own being.

Now comes the understanding that "man shall not live by bread alone," [1] but more by the consciousness of truth, that the acquisitive consciousness has given way to the I-have-meat-ye-know-not-of consciousness. In this consciousness, there is no selfhood for which to fear, since God has been revealed as the only Selfhood, Self-sufficient and eternal.

It now becomes apparent that life is lived by Grace as the gift of God, and the sense of personal effort, human will, and struggle falls away. Life is lived by the law of God. The supply of our daily needs unfolds, with no anxious thought, from the infinite source of Being. The divine harmonies of human relationships are maintained by the beauty and activity of the Soul—unless one forgets himself and temporarily becomes a reformer of others and, by so doing, brings on the enmity of the "natural man" who desires not at all to be extinguished.

[1] Matthew 4:4.

If we are rich, we are poor indeed unless our wealth is in Him. If we are well, the body aches unless our health is in Him. There is no peace, no security, and no joy except these be found in Him, whom to know aright is life eternal—yes, life, joyous, peaceful, and serene.

When the call comes to you to leave your "nets," you will understand that you are called upon to leave behind the limited and limiting sense of existence because you are ready to drop your dependence on persons, things, and conditions of the world to live wholly in God.

No longer will you so keenly love, hate, or fear the conditions of "this world," the realm of effect, because now you will perceive the true nature of God as the Cause, Law, and Source of your good. You will understand now that the Infinite Invisible is your rock, your fortress, your high tower, and your sanctuary from every storm and strife of human belief. Further than this, you will see that only the Invisible is power and, therefore, that no power for good or for evil exists in the realm of effect. Your entire obedience and dependence will rest upon the Within and not upon the without. When the Voice says, "I will make you fishers of men," [2] you will understand so clearly that God is your being that those who come to you will seek and find Spirit as their life, too.

Leave your "nets" and follow *Me*.[3]

[2] Matthew 4:19.
[3] The word "Me," capitalized, refers to God.

TWO

Knowing the Unknowable

Truth is infinite. Yes, truth is infinite, but that truth is within you. Then, how great is your capacity? How big are you? Infinite! Infinite, because infinity cannot be confined in anything less than infinity. Because of that, the true nature of your being is infinite, and from the depths of your being, infinity must flow. Nothing can be added to you: not even truth. Therefore, the only truth of which you can ever become aware is the truth that is already within your own being.

There are many ways of bringing truth to awareness and to conscious realization, bringing it into expression and activity. It is possible to retire to a mountain or a valley somewhere, take a little cabin for a month, six months, or a year or two, and just meditate day and night, and day and night, and day and night, remain alone, away from the world, carrying perhaps only a book of scripture, meditating, abiding in quietness and in peace, and praying and praying and praying. Eventually the truth that is within your own consciousness will begin to flow, to unfold, to come forth, and to reveal itself. In the end, if you are faithful and persevere, you will know all the truth that has ever been revealed since the dawn of civilization. That is one way.

Another way is through following some system of spiritual teaching in which there is a teacher with a measure of spiritual consciousness who, through his written or spoken word, is able to open the consciousness of those who come to him. One state of enlightened divine Consciousness can be to thousands desiring illumination what the sunlight is to the bud, opening it into the flower.

"I, if I be lifted up from the earth, will draw all men unto me." [1] "I, if I be lifted up" can draw all those who are searching and seeking to my level of consciousness. To no one does this apply more aptly than to the teacher of spiritual wisdom. The spiritual teacher can be a teacher only in proportion as he has received some measure of spiritual light—not because he has read books or because he knows and can recite statements of truth. Knowledge, as such, does not constitute a spiritual teacher. True, it may be one of the essential qualities of a teacher of mathematics, music, or engineering, but a spiritual teacher can impart only from the measure of his spiritual consciousness. And why? He is not going to teach truth at all. He is merely going to open consciousness so that the truth already within can flow forth.

When truth is recognized to be an integral part of your being, not even the search for truth will be left to you. How can you

[1] John 12:32.

seek and search for that which is already embodied within your own consciousness? You might as well say that you are a seeker for integrity or honesty, loyalty, fidelity, or morality. Are you seeking those things? Why not? Because you know that they are already embodied within you. Even if at this moment you are not manifesting the fullness of integrity, loyalty, fidelity, justice, and benevolence, even if you are not giving expression to these in their fullness, you know that they are within you and that you cannot go outside to get them.

And so it is with truth. So it is with family, companionship, home. There is no use to seek or to search for them because you will never find them. As a matter of fact, it should very quickly become evident to you that all seeking for things—all desire—is sin. You will soon recognize that every desire, even every good desire, is just an error that is separating you from your good. Why? Because the desire is for something you believe you do not have, but if or when you get it all will be well. If, however, the nature of your being is infinite, that cannot be true: you must already have it. It is already embodied within you, and as you learn to commune with the Father, it will begin to flow forth from you.

As a human being, you are limited: you can go no further in this life than your environment, education, or personal experience can carry you. You are subject to what the world calls laws: natural laws, laws of limitation, laws of matter, hereditary laws, medical laws, theological laws. Like a cork, floating on the ocean, you are a victim of every wave and every force that comes from every direction: from the water, from the wind above, and probably from beneath the water.

As a human being, man is always a victim and a target. He is forever being played upon by one kind of force or another: economic, political, the weather, climate, or food. If you permit yourself to live as a human being, you could live a life of continuous fear and doubt, a life of wondering what is going to happen next and from what direction it will come. As a matter of fact, that is the kind of life the world is living.

But it is not necessary for man to be a victim of the times, the tides, or conditions. By bringing himself into harmony with divine law, he becomes, not the victim of circumstances but, in the measure of his understanding, the master of them.

Throughout all time, the world has had the example of those great men—saints, seers, prophets, sages, or saviors—who made a direct and personal contact with the Source of all good. Furthermore, there is an extensive literature filled with accounts of those we might term average men and women who have also made that contact with their Source, and who then began to show it forth in their daily living, enabling them to be a blessing to all who came within range of their consciousness.

Unfortunately, at first the only medium these individuals had for imparting their experiences was through the spoken word, and for that reason only those who could personally come into the presence of the great masters of the past could receive the benediction or blessing of that contact. As the printing press brought about the wider dissemination of scriptural and other inspirational and spiritual literature, it became possible for more persons to have at least some contact with the letter of truth, and in a lesser degree even with the consciousness of the writers of truth. For that reason, during the last five hundred years many more persons have learned how to become at-one with the Infinite Invisible.

Today it is possible for anyone to bring divine Grace or the power of the Infinite into his individual experience and thereby be less limited and less dependent on human sources and resources than heretofore. More and more persons are now being

freed from the limitations of personal sense, that is, the limitations of their personal selfhood, than has ever been true in the
history of the world. But many as they are, it is not enough. The
possibilities are such that every person can be the outlet for this
love, Grace, power, and benediction, and there is no longer any
reason to restrict it to a few teachers or leaders, to a few saviors
or messiahs, or a few saints or seers.

At one time, it was believed that only those called to the religious life could enjoy this conscious union with God and that
through them their flocks could benefit vicariously. Today we
know that every man, woman, and child on the face of the globe
can leave their "nets" and bring themselves into that union,
thereby becoming a center or force through which God's grace
flows out into their community, speeding the day when the kingdom of heaven will be manifest on earth.

There comes a time in the experience of every person when
human circumstances are such that he realizes he cannot go any
further in the unfoldment of a happy, successful, or prosperous
life without the aid of something beyond humanhood; and it is
in such moments that he may turn to a search for what he calls
God. Some few there are who find God, but there are many
more who do not.

Probably the very word God keeps many persons from finding
Him because that word has been given so many meanings of a
superstitious nature that the way is often lost. In other words,
instead of seeing man made in the image and likeness of God,
what we usually do is to see God made in the image and likeness of man.

If we are to be successful in our search for God and attain
conscious oneness with our Source, we must go beyond the
mythical God of rewards and punishments, beyond faith in some
far-off Being who is but the figment of imagination and super-

stition. Probably if there were not so many false teachings about God, it would not be so hard to find Him. If we were wise enough to follow scriptural and mystical teachings, we would learn not to look outside for God, but to turn within until the revelation of the true God came from within our own being.

Did not Jesus teach that the kingdom of God is within, but have we not been making the mistake of praying to a God separate and apart from our own being? Is not every sense of discord in our experience, mental, physical, financial, and emotional, but a sense of separation from God? This sense of separation that we entertain is not of our making. That was done by religionists long, long ago. It was done by philosophers and by persons who were seeking God somewhere outside their own being, by those who were seeking good to be added to them.

The first lesson that we must learn, therefore, is that God is "closer . . . than breathing, and nearer than hands and feet." When we learn that, we begin to expect an unfoldment or revelation from within rather than a contact with Something outside of our being, unknown and afar off.

We must make the transition from the person who is seeking truth, seeking good, and seeking life eternal to that individual identity which is itself the source and center of infinite good, to the revelation of that individual identity which is the blessing—not receiving a blessing, but being it.

As we come into the realization of the true nature of our being and the true nature of God's being as individual being, in that proportion have we risen above the circumstances and conditions of human existence. At first this may leave us floating through space and wondering where we are going to land before we discover what this power of the Invisible is that acts upon our life and transforms our consciousness.

How many times have I said and written that, before we can

attain that which we are seeking, we must come to a place where we can see that which is invisible, hear that which is inaudible, and know that which is unknowable? "The things of the Spirit of God . . . are foolishness unto" [2] man.

This transformation of consciousness from the thinking mind to the intuitive will not come through the intellect, but rather it will define itself to what is called the Soul-faculties, the inner awareness. Jesus' statement, "Having eyes, see ye not? and having ears, hear ye not?" [3] is a reminder that we do not see spiritual truth or hear spiritual truth with the eyes or the ears. There is an inner consciousness, a spiritual faculty, that receives and interprets truth to us. We may call It [4] God, we may call It divine Love, universal Life, or the Spirit of God. Regardless of what name or term we use, however, we are acknowledging that there is a center of inspiration. We are acknowledging that of our own selves we can do nothing, that it is the Father within that does the works, that the Christ lives our life, meaning the Spirit of God in our individual being or individual awareness.

As we acknowledge that there is this infinite Source of inspiration and all good, we go on to the next step and realize that to the degree that that infinite good comes into our experience do we bring forth the beauty and bounty of that Infinity. Without It, we would be nothing; without It, we could do nothing.

Such a teaching is transcendental, and it is a reversal of the ordinary human sense of existence. For example, the world concept of supply is that we go out and get it, we work for it, plan, scheme for it, or steal; but in some way or other, we do get it.

---

[2] I Corinthians 2:14.   [3] Mark 8:18.

[4] In the spiritual literature of the world, the varying concepts of God are indicated by the use of such words as "Father," "Mother," "Soul," "Spirit," "Principle," "Love," and "Life." Therefore, in this book the author has used the pronouns "He" and "It," or "Himself" and "Itself" interchangeably in referring to God.

This teaching reverses that and says that the flow of the Spirit of God in us is the secret of supply. But this is something we could hardly go out and tell to the man on the street.

The world also believes that material remedies are absolutely essential, so would it not be foolish to try to tell anyone who places his faith in such remedies that, as effective as they may be, there is a more effective way? How many of them could understand that and accept such an idea? Why, it would be as ridiculous as saying that it is not necessary to pray to God for our good. I know because, when I have made that kind of a statement, I have seen the shock on the faces of persons who were well trained in religious beliefs. Not pray to God for our good? Unthinkable!

But how can we ask God for something that God must know we already need? Is not God omniscience, all-knowledge, all-wisdom? And if He is, is not the prayer that asks, begs, and beseeches God for the things of "this world" sin? The prayer, however, that turns to the Father and asks, "Open my eyes; illumine me; give me light. Be a light within me; shine through me; express. Fit me to be a better vehicle for Thy grace, a better servant of Thy will," comes nearer to the higher form of prayer which is communion with God.

It is like the relationship that exists between two persons who understand each other thoroughly, and who sit on a mountain or by a stream, looking at the scenery, enjoying the great delights of the mountains, the valleys, or the sea without any words passing between them, but looking at each other once in a while in mutual joy at this great privilege of beholding the work of God, two persons so completely in tune that just an occasional reminder, "Isn't the moon beautiful? Aren't the stars shining brightly tonight?" or a few words like that, and there is communion.

True prayer is like that. It is when one communes with God

and feels the divine Presence in him and through him, and in and through all people, and everything round about, and just smiles occasionally and exclaims, "Father, isn't this a heavenly earth we have here! Isn't this a beautiful world! Aren't people wonderful!"

That is the prayer of communion, and it comes about after we have attained a measure of life by Grace, a life in which God is fulfilling Itself as our experience.

It is not that God knows our material needs and supplies them. God knows nothing of our need for automobiles, typewriters, or washing machines. He probably does not even have an awareness of our need for employment. But God speaks to us in terms of fulfillment, and that fulfillment is always in terms we can understand. God speaks to us, and the mind interprets it in terms of dollar bills, books, employment, or companionship. God speaks as Spirit. We hear the Spirit, but we interpret It according to our needs, to that which makes for our fulfillment.

John tells us that God is love. If God is love, why ask God for love? God is love. God has no power to withhold love any more than God has power to withhold crops from the ground, or fish from the sea, or birds from the air. It is the function of Life to fulfill Itself, and that in infinite and abundant measure.

During the great depression of the thirties, churches all over the world were open day and night for those who wanted to pray to God for supply, and you know as well as I do that there was no lack of supply. The oceans were full of fish; Maine never was without a surplus of potatoes; the South never ran out of cotton; the Middle West always had more than enough cattle and wheat. As a matter of fact, these things were produced so abundantly that every day of the week thousands of railroad trains and scows were sent out laden with food to be thrown into the ocean or to be burned up. Crops were plowed under, and farmers were paid not to raise them; and all the time the churches were open day and night, filled with people praying for more supply. What would the world have done if God had been able to increase the supply? It would have had twice as much food to throw in the ocean and twice as much to burn up.

There was no sense in praying to God for supply then, and there is no sense in doing so now—unless we want to pray to Him to bring it to our back door for us in a truck. God is already producing more than the people of this earth are using. Yet, at this very moment, all over the world there are those who are praying for God to increase the supply on earth. If God doubled the amount of goods on earth, the people who are praying for it probably would not get any of it. All the prayers that have ever been sent up to God for more food or more clothing were just so much wasted wordage and wasted time.

There is a way to bring the infinity of supply into our experience, however, but that way is not by repeating a lot of words or singing sentimental songs, and by so doing believing that God is somehow going to begin giving us what up to now He has been withholding from us. No! No! That is not the way.

The way to restore normalcy, harmony, and abundance is not to pray to God to increase the supply, which is already greater than we can use, but rather to become consciously at-one with that Source so that it can flow. It is like the electricity which we use every day. There must be a contact with the source of the power before that power can flow and operate. The room in which we are sitting may be filled with electrical outlets; the walls may be lined with electrical wires; but it would do no good to sit around praying for electricity. The appliance must be plugged in before the power can flow.

So it is with us. God is the very life of our being, the very love and source of our being, but we must tune in. We must recognize and realize our at-one-ment. Our prayer then will never be a reaching out. It will never be an attempt to gain more truth, more life, or more love. It will never be a seeking of any form of demonstration—except one, and that is the demonstration of God's presence.

And so it is useless to pray any prayer in the sense of a desire to get, to accomplish, to achieve, or to demonstrate. The only legitimate prayer that will be left to us is a "Thank You, Father," and a sitting in the silence in sweet communion with the gentle Presence that is already within our own being. This Presence will not be added to us—no, no, no! It will be revealed as within our own being.

Do you see why desire is wrong? It is an acknowledgment of a lack. Jesus said, "Ask, and it shall be given you; seek, and ye shall find; knock, and it shall be opened unto you." [5] Beg, plead, knock, ask! But ask for Spirit, for spiritual illumination. Ask for God-realization, and pray for it. Ask for the gifts of the Spirit. Ask the Spirit for spiritual things. Paul said, "For we know not what we should pray for as we ought: but the Spirit itself maketh intercession for us." [6] Acknowledge then when you go to pray that you do not know what to pray for, and therefore what you are praying for is spiritual light, spiritual illumination.

Suppose that God could be so personalized as to be available to you here and now, what would you pray for? Something called a home, money, companionship, or a parking space? Or for the presence of God? If you were holding God's hand, would you not know that in the intimacy of that association God would know your need and provide for it? So the only thing you would pray for is God.

God really is just as available and tangible as though He were

[5] Matthew 7:7.   [6] Romans 8:26.

standing here visibly holding your hand. Why? Because God is omnipresent. God is omnipresence itself. God is the life and the fulfillment of all being. So if you have God, why do you have to ask for God *and* a parking place? If you have God, why do you have to ask for God *and* employment? Oh no, no! It would be enough to ask for God and get It. That would be enough for anyone—as all who have experienced God have found out. In the presence of God, there is nothing left for which to pray.

You profane prayer if you bring into it a concern, worry, fear, or a desire for anything or anybody. How can you believe in God and fear or doubt for the outcome?

From this moment on, then, you lose the privilege of praying for any person, any thing, or any condition. Your whole prayer becomes a continuous song of gratitude that God is love, that God is here, and that God is now. God is the all-knowing intelligence, the principle of our existence, the all-loving parent. Prayer thereby becomes a recognition of God's presence, a communion with God, a resting back in God's bosom, a holding of God's hand, a feeling of the divine Presence. That is prayer, and nothing else is.

Do you begin to see the reason for constant and frequent meditation? Do you see now why you require stillness of mind instead of taking thought? Do you see why in your meditation you must develop a listening attitude, a state of receptivity in which you do not think thoughts as much as wait for thoughts to come from the depths of your own being? Truth does not have to come from up in the sky. You do not have to strain for it. You do not have to make a mental effort for it. You merely have to let it gently flow forth.

Realize that all your good is to flow out from you. None of it can come to you. Divorce yourself from any outer dependence, whether person, place, or thing. See yourself in such a light that you can really and truly understand that if you walked out of your house in the morning without a dime in your pocket, you could fulfill yourself quickly with everything needful because it would not have to come to you but would flow out from you. If a bomb burst over the city, you would still go on eating three meals a day and have a place to sleep and be able to care for others. Out of what? Out of the depth of the infinite nature of your own Christhood. You could do as the Master did, walk out on the street and heal the sick and feed the multitudes. Out of what? Out of your Christhood. That is the lesson we all must learn: our Self-completeness in God and through God, our Self-completeness as the very Christ of God.

The truth which is your being becomes the light for all those who do not yet know that the kingdom of God is within them, and as they search for it they will find it through you. Not from you—no! You will be but the light revealing the light within them. You will never give them truth. The truth you will impart is the truth that is within them.

To a person of mortal, material consciousness it would seem impossible that a change could take place in his life by means of Something he had never seen, heard, tasted, touched, or smelled. But with that first experience would come more and more experiences, and as one change followed another, the day would come when somebody would say, "You know, you are not the same person I formerly knew." The transition from mortal, material sense to some measure of spiritual consciousness would have begun.

As these first experiences come, you realize that it is possible to bring about harmony, joy, and peace in the outer realm through spiritual means. However, you are still thinking in terms of dollar bills when you think of supply, only now you hope to accumulate them spiritually instead of materially. You are still thinking of a heart, lungs, liver, and gall bladder that operate in such and such a fashion, only now instead of bringing about their proper functioning through physical means, you are going to bring it about through spiritual means.

That was but the beginning of your transition from mortal, material sense to spiritual consciousness. But it was a transition, and that "old man" was beginning to "die," and a new one was being born, dependent on spiritual means for attaining material good.

The day eventually comes, however, when another transition has to be made, and the realization dawns that neither supply nor the body is material. Even the universe is not a structural universe.

"My kingdom is not of this world" [7]—no, not in any sense of the word. There are joys of which the people of this world have never even dreamed; there is a sense of health of which nobody in mortal or material sense, or even in the mental or half-way spiritual sense has ever conceived. There is another world, a new world. "My kingdom is not of this world": *My* [8] kingdom is the kingdom of heaven. There really is a heaven, and when the old earth and the old heaven are washed away, you come into the new earth and the new heaven and find that they are purely spiritual.

Now you enter a consciousness in which Spirit is your only health, your only supply. Now you do not think of using Spirit to get a human companion. You do not use Spirit to make the heart beat faster or slower, or to bring the pulse or blood pressure up or down. Here again is another transition; and in this second stage this man who has been "dying" for a long time is completely "dead." Now is he resurrected, probably more than

[7] John 18:36.
[8] The word "My," capitalized, refers to God.

resurrected: ascended into a divine state of consciousness in which the values are no longer earthly.

That transitional experience will go on and on and on until the ascension above all sense of this world. Then, there will be no more reincarnation because there will be no place into which to be reborn. The complete and perfect virginal, spiritual birth, or sense of being, will have been achieved. This is the "dying daily" and the rebirth that goes on continuously until the complete ascension.

THREE

Self-Completeness

————— ◄•► —————

You are Self-complete through God. You are not, and never will be, complete because of any effort you have ever made toward being good or being spiritual. Your completeness is in God. This is in accordance with the teaching of the Master Christ Jesus: "I can of mine own self do nothing.[1] . . . The Father that dwelleth in me, he doeth the works.[2] . . . Why callest thou me good? there is none good but one, that is, God.[3] . . . My doctrine is not mine, but his that sent me." [4]

In other words, all the power of Jesus was really the power of the Christ made evident through Jesus. Remember that, in

[1] John 5:30.   [2] John 14:10.   [3] Matthew 19:17.
[4] John 7:16.

and of yourself, you are nothing except that God be the reality of your being. Christ is your true identity, and in Christ you are fulfilled in all your completeness. So you can draw on your Christhood for anything to the extent of your realization of this truth.

> As the branch cannot bear fruit of itself, except it abide in the vine; no more can ye, except ye abide in me.
>
> John 15:4

Think of a tree with its trunk and its root system deep down in the earth, and then think of the branches on the tree. The tree has a root system which draws into it the food from the earth. It has a distributing system that sends that food up through the trunk out into the branches. There is a catalytic agent that turns the sun and the air and the water into some kind of an essence that feeds the branches and later becomes the fruit.

Now for a moment think of yourself as a branch, and realize how you are being fed: through the Trunk, or the Vine, from the Earth. As a human being, you are not partaking of that divine Substance: you are a branch cut off from the trunk of the Tree. It would appear that each of us is a separate unit, walking around in space, none of us attached to the other, none of us at one with the other, and certainly no sign of any God, feeding, supporting, maintaining, or supplying us: just ourselves, lone branches suspended in space, attached to nothing, and to outward appearances separate beings. That is the human picture.

If we use this illustration of the vine, however, we begin to perceive that although there seems to be a sense of separation, actually there is none. There are not three, roots, trunk, branches: there is only one. In other words, the word "tree" means branches, trunk, and roots: it does not mean just branches. We do not consider branches as the tree, or the trunk of a tree as the tree, or the roots as the tree; but when they are all assembled into one, then we call that a "tree."

Moreover, the life that flows through the roots into the trunk or vine and then out into the branches is the same life that later appears as blossoms and fruit. True, the branches and the trunk are visible, but we have to go beyond the visible in order to understand that there are roots and, too, there is the earth in which these roots are embedded, and it is through these roots that the minerals, moisture, and sunshine that permeate the earth are being drawn into the trunk and out into the branches by that which can never be seen: the Infinite Invisible which permeates all being.

At this moment, you are the branch that is visible; but you are one with the Vine, connected to this invisible Christ of your being, the connecting link with the Father, which in the tree-experience would be the life through which the tree draws its sustenance.

Surgery from head to foot will never reveal the Christ of your being because It is not physical. It would be as difficult to see as it would be to take a seed and dissect it in an attempt to find life in it. The life is not in the seed, and no one will ever find it there. The seed is embedded in life, and life flows in and out of the seed and around the seed and through it, always there in its dormant state, but always invisible.

Suppose you looked at the seed and refused to plant it because you could not see that there is an invisible life-force in that piece of inanimate matter. The seed, then, would remain a seed forever. But there is a life that acts upon the seed, in and through it, causing it to break open, to form, and to take root. There is an invisible life that does that. It is called *nature,* but nobody knows any more about the operation of nature than he knows about that of God. We simply take on faith the truth that there is life working in the seed, and that that life will appear outwardly as a plant. How readily we accept what we see in nature as having its source in what is not visible! How simple this is to understand!

Why are we not as willing to accept the truth that as branches of the Tree of Life we are not self-sustaining? Why do we continue to think of ourselves as separate human beings, each one dependent upon himself for his wisdom, supply, understanding, and intelligence, even for the health and strength of his body? Why do we never once think of this universal Life flowing as an invisible bond into and through each one of us, and realize that it is this Life-force that appears as the fulfillment of our life?

Without this Life pouring through us, we can do nothing. "Herein is my Father glorified, that ye bear much fruit" [5]—not a little, and not that we beg for it, not that we plead for it, not that we get on our knees and wonder why it is being kept from us.

God is glorified in that we bring forth much fruit. That glory cannot come, however, unless we can see that it is not our wisdom that produces it, nor our strength, nor our understanding, nor our learning, not even our business acumen or our ability in the world of economics and politics, but rather that whatever of good comes into our experience is the fruitage of that eternal Life. We do not beg for That; we do not plead for It; we do not pray for It: we open ourselves to Its flow.

If you have a continuous realization that the Life that flows through the Vine into you is flowing through every individual, you will find that that tie will quickly bring you into oneness with whatever is necessary for you. Can you not see that you would

[5] John 15:8.

need have no concern for your welfare even if you were out on the desert or in mid-ocean alone? Has anyone who has the conscious realization of his oneness with God ever feared, doubted, mistrusted, or had worries or concerns? If you could consciously realize your oneness with God, can you not see that you could drop all concern for the rest of your life?

It is only in the absence of your conscious oneness with God that you can fear. But it is a very foolish thing to say to anyone, "Oh, don't fear; give up your fear." Who can stop fearing as long as he thinks of himself as separate and apart from all other people and as separate and apart from God? Is it not true that every anxious thought you have ever had—every doubtful thought and every fearful thought—has been based on the belief that this outer part of you is all there is of your being, and that you had nothing to turn to except this finite being for your good, and that you knew what you wanted but did not know how to get it? In other words, does not every problem stem from a sense of separation from God?

How gloriously could the great teaching of the Master, "Take no thought for your life," [6] be fulfilled if at this moment you could accept the truth that the visible part of you is connected with an invisible link called the Christ, and that that invisible link is completely one with the Father, so that all that the Father has is flowing to you, the branch, through your Christhood!

The branch, then, will not go out and try to get fruit. No, every branch brings forth fruit from within itself. From within the branch? No, from within itself through its contact with the Vine and the Godhead: from the Father to the Christ, and from the Christ to the son.

Out of the Christ of your own being flows an infinity of good:

[6] Luke 12:22.

not that you of yourself have it any more than any other branch has, but that your oneness with the Christ, established in the beginning before ever the world began, is now consciously realized.

Whereas before you thought you were a separate entity who had to attract something to yourself from the outside, or pray to God and have God demonstrate something, now you see that the fruit will have to flow out from the depths of your own being, and appear outwardly—not come to you, not be hung on you as ornaments would be hung on a branch, and not be demonstrated, not achieved or accomplished by you, but permitted to flow out from you through the infinite nature of your Christhood.

Self-completeness through God! Do you see how self-complete a tree is, not by virtue of its being a tree, but because of its contact with the universal Life? Separate and apart from the ground, it would wither and die. Left rooted in the ground, it is a self-contained unit, drawing unto itself everything that it needs and producing it from the withinness to the without.

That is why all mystical literature has used the terms "within" and "withinness." It is not that the apples are inside the tree. They are not apples until they appear outside. But the essence or substance of the apples is flowing through the branches and becoming the form which appears as apples.

And so it is in every area of life. You do not have automobiles stored up inside of you, or dollar bills or houses or companions. Those you do not have within you. But you have the essence and the substance of them: you have the love and the life and the truth, the Spirit, the Soul, and the law. All these are within you; and flowing from within you, they appear outside as everything needful for your daily experience. One with your Father, you are a complete unit. One with your Father, you are Self-fulfilled through your conscious union with God.

Let me illustrate that in this way: Suppose you have a few loaves and fishes, but you have a multitude to feed, and you have no storehouses or barns. Now what can you do? Out of your humanhood, nothing. Starve! There is no alternative. But out of your Christhood, out of the depths of the infinity of your own being, you can look up and bless the loaves and fishes, realizing that these are not material loaves and fishes limited in number, but that this is God's supply, and if it is God's supply it is infinite.

Then the multitudes are supplied. Out of what? Your storehouse? No, out of the Father. The Father, the Christhood of you, is infinite, and out of It can flow whatever is necessary to your fulfillment. Out of It can flow millions of words, millions of ideas of truth. Why not millions of dollars, too? What is the difference? The source is the same; the substance is the same: in the beginning was God, and God was Spirit, and whether you call it loaves and fishes, dollars, or words of truth, everything that is comes forth from the Father, and so everything must be infinite. Only do not put one in the category of Spirit and the other in the category of matter.

Whatever measure of Christ has touched your consciousness has opened it to the great truth of the infinite nature of your being, of your Self-completeness in God, and to the recognition that nothing can be added to you and nothing can be taken from you. The more you give, the more you will have left. Pour out truth to the multitudes—only be sure that they are the multitudes who come to you in your mountain to seek it out. Then as they come, one by one, or come as multitudes, give it forth in the same way that you have received it, with the understanding that you are not giving anything to anyone: you are revealing to them that which is within their own being.

If once you see that this truth pouring forth is the substance of your loaves and fishes, of your protection, your safety, and your security, the fruitfulness of your entire experience will be established for all eternity: not only for threescore years and ten, but for eternity. You will, then, be the branch that bears fruit richly, Self-complete in God.

FOUR

Open Out a Way

———————◆————————

Since there seems to be a sense of separation between the Father
and us, and between all those who are to play a part in our life's
experience, our work is to realize our oneness with the Father,
the one Consciousness, and then we automatically become one
with every spiritual being. There is but one Consciousness, and
that Consciousness, functioning as your consciousness and as
mine, is the connecting link between you and your world and
me and my world, establishing us in oneness with all those who
are a part of our fulfillment.

Unless we wish to engage in a daily battle of competition, a
daily battle of trying to work with persons antagonistic to our
ideas, unless we wish to take our chance with whether we will

have the right employer or right employee, or whether we will deal with those who are the right people for us or the wrong— unless we wish to do that, we must establish firmly our oneness with the Father before we leave our home in the morning to embark upon any enterprise, commercial, social, or ministerial, realizing that the consciousness of the Father, which is our consciousness, is the consciousness of every individual. Therefore, all those ready for the experience of association with us, by the attraction of that Consciousness, are brought to us, and in the same way, we are led to everyone we can serve or bless.

When we understand our connection with the Vine, we do not compete with any man. We do not fight, we do not war with him or sue him because we have access to the infinite Source of our being, and it is this Source that feeds and supplies us even while it is feeding and supplying all the other branches on the tree.

So instead of looking to one another for our needs, we learn to look to the one universal Life that is flowing through all of us, and receive our good from It. Then everything works together for good, and we are led to where we can work with others, benefit from and cooperate with them, and yet not live off them.

Let us assume, for a moment, that you are the branch, and that I stand in relationship to you as the Vine, the teacher who has in some measure realized this relationship of oneness. You come to me for inspiration, guidance, teaching, or healing. You know that of my own self I can do nothing. You know that as a human being I have no more power to give you any of those things than you have to give them to me. But you are not concerned with me as a person: you are concerned only with the degree of enlightened consciousness which I represent, and that enlightened consciousness is the Vine.

So you come to me, the Vine, and because of my recognition of my oneness with the Source and my years of experience in contacting It, understanding and awareness flow through this Vine to you. You can come to me or go to any spiritual teacher, and through that enlightened consciousness receive some measure of good. The measure is not always the same, but whatever measure of good you receive from the person who at the moment represents the Vine is only because he has attained a state of consciousness a step ahead of you who are seeking help.

Any person, rooted and grounded in God and living consciously in oneness with his Source, serves as the Vine for the branches: those looking to him for help. It must be remembered, however, that this relationship is only a temporary one because every individual must learn that he, too, is the Vine for those who are the branches in his experience.

Today the world is filled with people hungry for spiritual enlightenment, and because they are so hungry, so ready, and are seeking, they must find a Vine. They must make contact with a state of spiritual illumination that will reveal that they, too, can draw forth rich fruitage from the infinite Source within. For this reason, therefore, you must be the Vine to those finding their way into this spiritual union.

At this point, you may think of yourself as a branch, but through meditation, study, and devotion, as you learn to leave your "nets," you come to the place where your relationship to the world is as a Vine, not as a branch. You will recognize yourself as rooted and grounded in the infinite Source of good, and therefore, willing and ready to let that good of God flow through you that those who turn to you may be fed and may, in their turn, be enabled to bring forth fruitage.

Whatever of good comes into your experience is not for your

good or mine: it is that the Father may be glorified through us. The egotistical sense of life that has resulted in men and women thinking how great or how supreme in wisdom they are is a destructive force to themselves and to our very civilization. The realization that we are instruments for that Divinity that is manifesting Itself and Its glory as our individual being brings the fruitage of health, harmony, wholeness, peace, and joy into our experience, God expressing Itself as these qualities.

Our outer experience is an expression of our inner state of consciousness. To the person who has no consciousness of sin, sin would be an impossibility. To the person who has been brought up to abhor blasphemy or obscene language, the use of such words is completely foreign to his nature; they just do not enter his thought or drop from his lips because they are no part of his consciousness. On the other hand, those who have lived in an environment of grossness where loose language holds sway find it a very simple matter, and not at all shocking, to use all kinds of vulgarities of speech. This they could not do unless it were a part of their consciousness.

In every walk of life throughout all time, it has been the same. One person is a good businessman, and his next door neighbor a poor one. Naturally, the poor businessman would like to be a good one, but there seems to be something in his state of consciousness preventing it. There have been many salesmen who wanted to be good ones who never achieved their goal—not that they did not have the desire, but because they did not have the necessary state of consciousness. There have been good statesmen and bad ones, and the bad ones certainly wanted to be good ones. Always the inner state of consciousness appears outwardly as one's daily experience.

Humanly, the only way to rise above being an unsuccessful salesman, a poor businessman, or an ineffectual statesman is to do as much as possible to educate oneself. That, of course, has its limitations since one cannot educate himself or study to any greater extent than his state of consciousness permits. One person may be able to study eight hours a day with profit, and the other cannot study even one hour a day and absorb anything. This, too, represents the state of consciousness of the individual.

There is a way to surmount these difficulties and break down every limitation, and that is in the realization of this inner spiritual life as individual consciousness. Then, instead of being limited to our personal experience, education, or ability to study, we will begin to understand the nature of our being, and as we do, we will find that this universal Consciousness is really our true being.

The kingdom of God is within us, and because this kingdom of All-good is within we must stop looking for love to come to us, stop looking for gratitude, recognition, or reward. These are qualities that must flow out from us. Strange, is it not, how we have looked everywhere for love, appreciation, gratitude, cooperation, and reward—everywhere except where they actually exist, within our own being?

This looking outside is what has separated man from his good. He has been trying to draw good to himself from outside: either praying for it or trying to have it brought to him from somebody else, and if not from somebody else, then from God. The fact that it does not come does not seem to change such a person's attitude. In fact, it reinforces the attitude of looking outside for good by adding frustration to it.

But we must now cease looking to any person for good—even for integrity, loyalty, or fidelity; we must let those qualities flow out from us. Then, as they are expressed to us in our relationship with others, we will be experiencing what we have already loosed into the world. The love, reward, gratitude, justice, mercy, or kindness that we let flow out from us is the only love, justice, mercy, kindness, or gratitude that can ever flow back to us.

Some of you are still seeking health, and I can tell you that you will never find it. Health is already established within you, or else there is no God. What would you think of a God who had the power to give health to you and was withholding it from you? Personally, I cannot believe in a God who has that power, and yet withholds it until I find the right words with which to pray, or the right medicine. No! No! God has established within His son health, harmony, wholeness, and peace, but we have missed the fruitage of God by looking for these outside our own being: in medicine bottles, in prayers or treatments. They do not exist out there. Wholeness, harmony, completeness, perfection, all are within you. You must find some way to open up an avenue for these to flow out from you.

You are keeping yourself from the experience of happiness, joy, and peace by looking for them and expecting them to come to you. They will not! They will not! But you can bring them into your experience by opening up your consciousness and letting them flow out.

If you do not have enough love in your life, let more love flow out. Do not look around and expect the other person to bring it to you. If you are not experiencing enough reward or recognition in your work, gratitude for your services, or appreciation of your value, do not look to anyone for it: not to man, not to God.

A human being is cut off from his supply of good by the belief that it is separate and apart from his own being. The son of God is he who understands that he is that avenue, instrument, or vehicle through which the infinite nature of God's being is pouring Itself. It is he who knows that the Father is glorified in his bringing forth much fruit: not getting it from somebody, but bringing it forth from within his own being.

Every desire to get good is but one more stumbling block in your path of getting it, just another form of separation barring it from you. Only in the realization that God has established Its good within you and that you are the means of Its flowing out to the world can you achieve your freedom. Only in the sense of your Self-completeness as the revealed son of God do you find yourself coming into possession and realization of all good on the outer plane.

As you realize God to be the Source of your protection, safety, and security, you do not look to bomb shelters, to armies or navies: you look to the Source for safety, security, peace, and joy. And that Source is within your own being. Therefore, you meditate, you go within so as to realize that within your consciousness—not within your body—is the completeness of being, and you are opening out a way for it to flow forth, not a way for it to come to you. This is a complete reversal of the human picture.

"In thy presence is fulness of joy." [1] When you begin to acknowledge that Presence, you begin to acknowledge the presence of the fullness of life. "I am come that they might have life, and that they might have it more abundantly." [2] The moment you acknowledge the presence of that *I*,[3] you are acknowledging fulfillment. It has not sent you out into the world to fulfill anything or to get fulfillment from the world: It has come to fulfill Itself, and you are to get your fulfillment from that *I* at the center of your being.

The longer you look outside for love, wisdom, justice, recognition, and reward, the longer you separate yourself from the ex-

[1] Psalm 16:11.   [2] John 10:10.
[3] The word "*I*," italicized, refers to God.

perience of them. You have not come into this world to *get* love, justice, kindness, or mercy from another: you are here to draw it forth from that which is your fulfillment. The fullness of the Presence means the fullness of life.

Begin your day by recognizing the presence of God, the *I* that is come to fulfill. Withdraw your gaze from the outer world, and then after that go about your business. Go to your office in the realization of this inner Consciousness as being your fulfillment, and look neither to employer nor employee. Your good may come through them, but it will come through them only as you recognize that it is coming from within your own being. To *look* to them for it is the mistake. Expecting good from others is the sin. As long as you do not look to another for your good, good will flow to you.

You are not a human being at the mercy of time, tide, circumstance, or condition. You are the child of God, fed from the infinite springs of water within your own being. You have now come to a place in consciousness where you must realize as did Jesus: " 'I have meat to eat that ye know not of.' [4] I have an inner Source of good; I can give you waters, living waters that spring up into life everlasting."

You begin now to live in the New Dimension of life in which you are not the receiver of good, but rather the avenue through which good flows out to the world. You do not have to resort to the trickeries and treacheries of human existence for your well-being. You do not have to take thought for your life. Now you can live in a dimension of life that realizes: "Your Father knoweth that ye have need of these things. . . . for it is [His] good pleasure to give you the kingdom" [5]—to let it flow through you, not only to feed you, but to feed five thousand.

[4] John 4:32.   [5] Luke 12:30,32.

Do not ever forget that! There is not a person of illumined consciousness who could not feed a whole city if only he would realize that it is not out of his own storehouse that it must come, but from the depths of those Wellsprings within.

Never hesitate in the days to come to let the world draw upon you. Do not withhold good in any form from those who seek it, whether it is a word of wisdom or a dollar bill, whether it is food, clothing, health, safety, or security. Do not withhold! No matter how much you pour out, you will not impoverish yourself because it is not out of your storehouses or barns that you are giving: it is out of the infinity of the universal Source.

This is the New Dimension where you permit the world that does not yet know its true identity to call on you as an avenue for the Infinite. This is where the world must begin to try to find what it is looking for in the form of world peace. There cannot be world peace while a nation believes that its good is dependent on some other nation, or on attaining more land or greater natural resources. Just as you individually must come to that place in consciousness where you realize that you can draw on the infinite Storehouse, so must the nations of the world come to a place where they no longer try to get their good by warring for it.

Today you begin the rebirth. You "die" today. You "die" today to the human being seeking good. You must be reborn of the Spirit of God into the realization of good flowing forth through you. Pray? Yes, yes! Pray without ceasing, but do not ask, beseech, or beg God. No, no! Prayer must now be an inner communion with the Source of all good. It must not be asking for things; it must be a recognition that at the center of your being there is this invisible Vine which has been placed there in the beginning in order that you might be fulfilled. Then your good will appear in the outer realm in whatever form is necessary.

As circumstances and conditions arise in human experience,

wherein it appears that you are separated from your good, remember:

I will never leave thee, nor forsake thee.

Hebrews 13:5

When thou passest through the waters, I will be with thee; and through the rivers, they shall not overflow thee: when thou walkest through the fire, thou shalt not be burned; neither shall the flame kindle upon thee.

Isaiah 43:2

Only be courageous. Fear not; doubt not! *I* will never leave you, nor forsake you. In moments of trial, tribulation, stress, doubt, or fear, bring to your conscious realization the truth that good cannot come to you.

Learn to stand still in quietness and in confidence with that inner assurance given in the Twenty-third Psalm: "The Lord is my shepherd; I shall not want." [6] The Lord is your shepherd— *is,* no begging, no beseeching; *is.* "Yea, though I walk through the valley of the shadow of death, I will fear no evil." [7] Why? "Thou art with me." [8] Even in the valley of the shadow of death, in the midst of trial, tribulation, or distress, in the midst of any sinful or sick experience, remember it is only being prolonged through a sense of separation from God. You can end it, and you can end it quickly.

Bring to conscious remembrance the fact that in spite of these appearances, even that of death, you need not fear, since the *I* that has come to fulfill you is still present. "I will never leave thee, nor forsake thee.[9] . . . Son, thou art ever with me, and all that I have is thine.[10] . . . I will go before thee, and make the crooked places straight." [11]

[6] Psalm 23:1.   [7] Psalm 23:4.   [8] Psalm 23:4.
[9] Hebrews 13:5.   [10] Luke 15:31.   [11] Isaiah 45:2.

In every book of the Bible can be found some character who had a measure of awareness of God as the divine infinite Presence, and it was that Presence that enabled him to be the prophet, saint, sage, or seer of his day. Every individual on the face of the globe today who attains some measure of realization of that Presence also becomes the sage, saint, prophet, seer, or savior of this day, and this is revealed as a universal relationship possible to everyone.

"Greater works than these shall he do." [12] Any works that have been done on the spiritual path will be repeated, and repeated even in greater measure, but only in proportion to the realization of this Presence. Any sense of separation from your good or any attempt by prayer to bring good to you must result in an even greater sense of separation, a greater sense of lack and loss. Begin today to make the transition from the human being seeking good to the state of divine being that knows itself to be the outlet and avenue for all of God's grace to the world.

I have set my seal upon you. I have made you in my own image and likeness. I have bestowed upon you divine Grace and freedom that you might be the child of God.

I have made you a leader of men, a fisher of men. I have glorified you with the glory that I had with the Father in the beginning. I have called you by My *name. Call upon* Me *and be saved. Look unto* Me. *Abide in* Me *and let* My *word abide in you.*[13]

---

[12] John 14:12.

[13] The italicized portions of this book are spontaneous meditations which have come to the author during periods of uplifted consciousness and are not in any sense intended to be used as affirmations, denials, or formulas. They have been inserted in this book from time to time to serve as examples of the free flowing of the Spirit. As the reader practices the Presence, he, too, in his exalted moments, will receive ever new and fresh inspiration as the outpouring of the Spirit.

As you listen to that still small voice within your being, you are fed from an inner Spring. You are housed, clothed, maintained, sustained, protected, and divinely influenced, "not by might, nor by power, but by my spirit." [14]

"In quietness and in confidence shall be your strength." [15] There is no struggle. You are not battling for your good: the battle is not yours, so be still! Be still and know, and you will hear a voice within you say, "*I* am God." Why from within you? Because the kingdom of God is within you, and God is in His kingdom, and from that Kingdom within you God announces and declares Himself so that you need not battle or struggle for a living or for health.

The battle is not yours: it is God's. Only acknowledge God as the Source, the Power, the Presence, and as the Revelator of all good; and above all, here and now, in this place, at this time, give up seeking for love, peace, joy, power, dominion anywhere, at any time. Acknowledge that these qualities flow forth through you, and that the Source of them, the kingdom of God, is within you. Because of that, this entire world may draw upon you at any moment for health and wealth, and you will answer, "Here it is"—not counting first how much you have in your pocket, storehouse, farm, or bank, but realizing that whatever it is that is to go out is to go out through you from the kingdom of God.

[14] Zechariah 4:6.
[15] Isaiah 30:15.

F I V E

Hidden Manna

—◄●►—

Ours is a New Dimension. We do not seek the world: we abide at the center of our own being, behold the glory of God, and let the world come to us.

> He that hath an ear, let him hear what the Spirit saith unto the churches; To him that overcometh will I give to eat of the hidden manna.
>
> Revelation 2:17

"He that hath an ear"—he that hath an inner ear, he that hath a spiritual ear, he that can hear what is not audible—let him hear. Let him hear what the Spirit says—not what I say, not what the book says, not what you would like to say to your neighbor, but what the Spirit says—"To him that overcometh will I give to eat of the hidden manna."

The whole import of the message of The Infinite Way could well be summed up in that term "hidden manna." Hidden manna! How like that expression is to that other statement of the Master's: "My peace I give unto you: not as the world giveth, give I unto you": [1] not physical health or material wealth, a home or an automobile, not anything that the world gives, but *My* peace. *My* peace is something that the world would not recognize if it came face to face with it, and would not realize even if it experienced it. *My* peace: a peace that comes, not because the body is healthy or the purse is full, not because the home is happy, prosperous, or joyous! No, no, no! *My* peace is a state of peace that is experienced within, regardless of outside conditions, but which ultimately changes the outside conditions.

Here you have a hidden mystery. Peace, such as the world gives, comes to you because of external circumstances or conditions. If you have more health or wealth, a bigger home, or a longer vacation, that may induce a temporary state of peace, but this good that comes to you from the external world today may be taken from you tomorrow. *My* peace is different from that. *My* peace is an inflow and an outflow from within your own being, and so it is never dependent on anything: it is self-created, self-maintained, and self-sustained. *My* peace comes from a hidden spring within, and when it comes, the good that it brings will never leave you.

In other words, the peace that is realized within will forever establish harmony in your outer world. This is the hidden manna; this is the meat to which the Master referred when he said, "I have meat to eat that ye know not of." [2] That was the

---

[1] John 14:27.   [2] John 4:32.

hidden meat, the spiritual meat. When he said, "Man shall not live by bread alone, but by every word that proceedeth out of the mouth of God," [3] he referred to that spiritual bread, that spiritual supply and substance—not to outer bread or outer circumstances.

The world seeks peace, harmony, wholeness, and contentment, but it is seeking them from something that it first thinks it must acquire externally in the outer realm. True, it may even enjoy that peace, prosperity, and contentment as long as the particular circumstance or condition lasts, but usually it loses satisfaction in what it has gained in the outer, as if it were a toy, and soon it looks around for a new toy.

Life becomes entirely different once you catch hold of the great truth that the "word that proceedeth out of the mouth of God" is the substance of life, and understand the meaning of those mystical passages of Scripture.

> I have meat to eat that ye know not of.
>
> John 4:32

> If thou knewest the gift of God, and who it is that saith to thee, Give me to drink; thou wouldest have asked of him, and he would have given thee living water. . . .
> Whosoever drinketh of the water that I shall give him shall never thirst.
>
> John 4:10, 14

> I am the bread of life.
>
> John 6:35

> To him that overcometh will I give to eat of the hidden manna.
>
> Revelation 2:17

As you begin to see that that which is outward and tangible and visible is but the product of that which is invisible, you will

[3] Matthew 4:4.

not judge your supply by how many apples or peaches or dollars you have, but by how much God-contact you have.

Whatever good is to appear in your life must appear as the result of the activity of truth in your consciousness. In other words, if your consciousness is the same tomorrow as it is today, you cannot expect any fruits tomorrow different from what you had today. In order to have a different experience tomorrow there must be some kind of a different activity in your consciousness today. If you are to bring spiritual fruits into your experience, you must leave your "nets" and purge yourself of whatever branches you are holding onto that are dead.

You will not be able to enter the presence of God carrying your burdens with you. You will not come into the presence of God carrying with you any desire for God to do something, be something, or get something for you. There has to be a purification of all human desires in the realization of His grace. You must consciously make the sacrifice of everything external; you must surrender the past and the future. Surrender every desire for person, place, thing, circumstance, or condition—even your hope for heaven.

The presence of God is within you, and it must be consciously realized, but it will never be realized by anyone who desires God for any purpose other than the realization of God Itself. Everyone who has sought God and missed the way has missed it because he has sought God for a reason: for a healing, for supply, for a home, for happiness, or for some other thing. God cannot be attained that way. God can be attained only in one way: through a complete surrender of everything except the one desire to bask in that Grace that is sufficient unto you.

Think what it would mean to have that Grace. Think what it would mean to have the peace of the Christ, the *My* peace that the Christ can give unto you, not the peace of the world, not health or money, not position, place, or power: only spiritual peace. Think what it would mean if you could desire only *My* peace, the Christ-peace, with no thought of what it would do or what it would get for you!

Only in proportion as you consciously do this within your own consciousness will it be so unto you. Consciously let go and say, "I do not want to live by bread alone. I want my life to be lived 'by every word that proceedeth out of the mouth of God.' " Then the miracle will follow.

When you have divested yourself of material and human dependencies, such words as "you," "he," and "she" will diminish and almost fade out of your vocabulary. No longer will you think so much about the "you," the "he," or the "she" from whom you are expecting so much. Now as the needs arise in your experience, the first thought will be the Christ. From the Christ, and through the Christ, will all good appear: not through you, not through any "he," "she," or "it," only through the Christ.

True, the Christ will appear as some human avenue. Your good can come to you through me, and my good can come to me through you, but mine will not come *from* you, and yours will not come *from* me. I will never look to you, and you will never look to me. I will look to the Christ of my being, and then the Christ of my being will appear as you. And you will look only to the Christ of your being for truth, and today that may appear as me. Tomorrow it will appear as someone else, but it will always be the Christ of your own being appearing to you.

As less and less you personalize your good and the avenues through which your good is to come, and let the Christ appear as whatever form is necessary to your experience at the moment, more and more you will find it will be so unto you. As you re-

alize the Christ to be the source and the fount of your good and
continuously look to It, thus will It flow.

There are times when you may wonder, "Do I deserve this
good? Am I worthy of it? Do I have sufficient understanding to
receive it? Do I have time to do all the study and reading and
praying necessary for this good?" And so I would like you to
know that none of this is dependent upon anything that you may
do. It is the pure activity of the Christ to which you open yourself.

Nothing can stay God's hand, not even your sins of omission
or commission. Nothing you can do, or ever have done, will prevent the flow of God. It is not dependent on how much reading,
church-going, studying, and how much meditating you do. All
these are merely aids to opening your consciousness. That is the
only function they play. God is not sitting around waiting for
you to become good or spiritual, or until you have read so many
hundred pages of truth, or meditated for so many hours.

The Christ is the reality of your being now. It is there waiting,
but it is you who must let It in: first by purging yourself of the
belief that It is something outside your being; then secondly, by
your letting It flow through your realization of Its omnipresence.

If you believe for a second that your good is dependent on
anything that you may humanly do or leave undone, you bar
yourself from the flow of God. God Itself is flowing forth infinitely, and the only barrier to the fullness of Its expression is
in proportion as you might accept the belief that the good of
God is dependent upon what you do or leave undone. Any spiritual activity in which you may engage is not for the purpose of
gaining the good of God: it is for the purpose of enabling you to
learn how to open your consciousness to the inflow.

Do not believe that you can either bring about the flow of
God or prevent Its flow. It is already full and complete within

your being, awaiting your recognition of your fullness in Christ. Though your sins be scarlet, you are white as snow. Only do not go back; do not sin again; do not go back to the belief of a sense of separation from God. Do not go back to seeking your good from outside because after you have learned that the kingdom of God is within you and that you must let it flow up from the within to the without, if you then again go seeking it without, you create a deeper sense of separation than you ever had before. Do not do it! Do not go back! Do not go back! "Go, and sin no more." [4] Do not go back to being hurt because somebody is not doing for you what you think he should: forgiving you, co-operating with you, or recognizing your virtues. Do not go back to that! Loose him! Forgive him and let him go! You are alone with your God. You are alone in your God-being.

There are times when you are faced with the appearance of discord, inharmony, pain, lack, or limitation; and the temptation is to make a mental effort to indulge in vigorous thought-taking, affirmations, and denials in order to achieve peace and harmony.

Now reverse that, and whenever there is an appearance of discord, relax. Make no mental effort. Remember that your good does not come to you by might or by power, but by the very gentle Spirit. It does not come to you by your striving, by your efforts, by your thought-taking: it comes to you from the depths of your being, in stillness, in quietness, and in confidence.

You are not to try to achieve a healing. You are to be still and let the still small voice take over. You are to let the Spirit descend upon you. Rest. Rest, right now, in the midst of the disease, lack, discord, or inharmony that is disturbing you. Rest; relax!

[4] John 8:11.

"My grace is sufficient for thee.[5] *. . . I will never leave thee, nor forsake thee."* [6] *Why struggle as if you had to hold on to Me? Why struggle as if you had to seek for Me and search for Me? I am in the very midst of thee, "closer. . . . than breathing, and nearer than hands and feet."*

If you know how to give good gifts to your children, how much more do I, your heavenly Father, know? Do not struggle for them. I will give them to you. I will give you water: do not lower buckets for it. Do not strive. I will give you water. You, you be still. Let Me feed you. Let Me satisfy your thirst. Let Me, at the center of your being, be the healing influence, the healing Christ.

Do not try to make your mind or your thoughts the healing Christ. "My thoughts are not your thoughts, neither are your ways my ways." [7] *Why do you not give up your thoughts and give up your ways? Let My thoughts take over. You just rest and listen to Me—the still small voice at the center of your being.*

I will never leave you. I will never forsake you. Even in "the valley of the shadow of death," [8] *I will be there. You will never know death; you will never die. Why? Because I give you living waters that spring up into life everlasting.*

And so if you are listening for My still voice, if you are resting in My everlasting arms, if you are relaxing in Me, if you are letting every word that proceedeth out of My mouth feed you, maintain and sustain you, you will never die.

I have never known a righteous man to beg bread. What is a righteous man? Only he who rests in his union with Me. Rest, then, in the contemplation of My love and My presence. My Spirit is with you. My presence goes before you.

"In my Father's house are many mansions. . . . I go to pre-

5 II Corinthians 12:9.   6 Hebrews 13:5.
7 Isaiah 55:8.   8 Psalm 23:4.

pare a place for you." [9] I *do. Stop thinking, then. Stop, stop, stop fearing; stop doubting. Stop trying to hang on to sentences and words and affirmations and denials. Let go; rest in* My *bosom; rest in* My *arms. I, your heavenly Father, know that you have need of these things, and it is* My *good pleasure to give them to you—not make you struggle and strive for them, not make you treat for them, but give them to you through Grace. Not by might, not by power, but by* My *spirit. You can do all things through* Me, *the Christ of your being.*

Let the Christ be the avenue through which you are fed, clothed, housed, and comforted, healed, protected, maintained, and sustained. Whenever an appearance of discord comes upon your horizon, relax more, rest more, be more at peace in the assurance of the divine Presence within you. Trust the *I,* trust the Christ at the center of your being.

Believe that there is a Presence whose only function is to bless you, to be a benediction to you, and to be the instrument of God's grace. Trust It. "Put not your trust in princes" [10]—believe only in God. Do not live by bread any longer, at least not by bread alone, but by every word, every promise of Scripture which must be fulfilled in you: "Whither thou goest, I will go.[11] . . . To him that overcometh will I give to eat of the hidden manna." [12]

That manna is hidden within you. It is invisible to the world, unknowable to common sense, incomprehensible to human beings. It is hidden from the world. Where is it hidden? In the depths of your own being.

Take your attention away from the men and women of the world. Take your dependence and faith away from the people

9 John 14:2.   10 Psalm 146:3.
11 Ruth 1:16.   12 Revelation 2:17.

of the world and the circumstances and conditions of the world, and remember only this: Deep down within you there is a meat that the world does not know; there are untapped springs of water and hidden manna, and all of this is embodied within your own being.

S I X

The New Name

————◆•▸————

"To him that overcometh"—more especially to him who over-
comes that desire to seek and to search in the outer realm—
"will I give to eat of the hidden manna, and will give him a white
stone, and in the stone a new name written, which no man
knoweth saving he that receiveth it." [1] What is that name?
Christ. No more are you Jones, Brown, or Smith; no more are
you "man, whose breath is in his nostrils"; [2] no more are you a
man seeking good; no more are you a prodigal, separate and
apart from the Father's house. Now your name is Christ.

Is there anything for the Christ to receive? Or is the Christ
that which feeds and heals the multitudes, that which restores

[1] Revelation 2:17.   [2] Isaiah 2:22.

and resurrects, that which is, in and of Itself, the Kingdom of all harmony?

A new name you receive: no longer man. But would you tell your friends that you are the Christ? No! Never voice such things as "I am God," "I am spiritual," "I am the Christ," or "I am the son of God." Do not ever do that! It would not be true. It would be just the same as going around and saying, "I am honest; I am moral; I am good." You could hardly do that, and if you did, I am afraid your neighbors might suspect you. And they would certainly have every right to suspect you if you ever said, "I am the Christ."

Only once or twice did the Master reveal his true identity. He was very, very careful about that. Even when Pilate asked him, "Art thou the King of the Jews?" Jesus' answer was, "Thou sayest." [3] He did not say it!

All life is a matter of choices. "Choose you this day whom ye will serve." [4] If you choose, you can remain "man, whose breath is in his nostrils." If you choose, you can continue your search for good, your search for supply, your search for eternality and for immortality. You can continue your search for peace, and sometime or other you may stumble upon it or it may be brought to you. Or you can give up your search this very moment: you can give up your desire for good; you can give up all expectation of good this day; and you can rest back in your true name, in your divine sonship.

The Prodigal Son in his divine sonship had everything: a luxurious home, loving parents, understanding friends, and an enviable position in life. Then came that sense of separation that sent him out into the world to achieve something on his own, probably the desire to be something of himself. In a short while,

---

[3] Matthew 27:11.   [4] Joshua 24:15.

he had used up his substance, the supply that had been stored up, but which was now not renewing itself because it no longer had contact with its Source, his Father's house. At the end of the road came the realization that even the servants were better off than he. Then began the return to the Father's house, but while yet a long way off, the Father came to greet him and re-establish him in his heirhood, and all was well again. Why? Just because of his return to the Father's house, to the Father-consciousness.

Human beings are all "prodigals." The prodigal-state is actually a sense of separation from God, or what in theology is known as the Fall of Man. It is the descent from the divine Consciousness to the belief and acceptance of a selfhood apart from God; whereas the return to the Father's house is but a remembrance that God is their selfhood, God is their true identity and their true being.

The Prodigal came home and because of his sonship received the purple robe, the ring, and the jewels. You, too, can return to the Father's house tonight, and even while you are quite a distance away from the realization of it, the Father is on His way out to meet you, and to place upon your shoulders that purple robe of divinity, that jeweled ring of dominion over the earth and all that is therein, over the sea, and over the air, that ring which denotes spiritual authority—a new stone, a new gem with a new name: Divine Son.

If you accept this truth, no longer will you waste your time or energy in searching for things or persons, but you will rest in the realization of your divine sonship and *let* your good unfold, *let* it come to you. You must realize that it never will come to you from outside your own being: it must unfold to you from within.

Now your expectancy is from that hidden manna that you can

share with those not yet aware of their new name. Now you abide in your sonship and say, "Come to me," but silently—not on a street corner, not to the neighbors—silently, " 'Come unto me, all ye that labour and are heavy laden, and I will give you rest.' [5] *I* will give you peace; *I* will feed you; *I* will give you living waters; *I* will share with you this hidden manna." Now you know where all supply is to be found: it is hidden within you. It cannot come to you: it must flow out from you to the world.

As a prodigal, you are out in the world seeking, working, striving, getting. As the Divine Son, the world comes to you to share in the riches which are yours by inheritance. A new word now, inheritance. Inheritance! "Not by might, nor by power," [6] but as the child of God are you heir of God, joint-heir with Christ to all the heavenly riches.

Can you imagine Jesus praying for health or supply for himself or anyone else? This he never did because he was completely aware of his divine sonship. There was no need for him to receive anything; there was no way for him to receive more than he had because all that the Father had was already his. And all that the Father has is already yours. Ah! but after you have declared, "All that the Father has is mine," are you one of those who then continues praying for more: for supply, understanding, friendship, or companionship? Do you think any prayer is necessary after you have realized your divine sonship and your relationship to God? No, there is only one thing then: stand steadfast in truth; remain faithful in the understanding of the truth you have received.

Every revelator of spiritual truth has known that I am *I,* that I am *He,* that *I AM* is God; that *I* is the only God there is.

[5] Matthew 11:28.   [6] Zechariah 4:6.

When thou passest through the waters, I will be with thee; and through the rivers, they shall not overflow thee: when thou walkest through the fire, thou shalt not be burned; neither shall the flame kindle upon thee.

Isaiah 43:2

You will not drown, because *I* will go with you—*I*. That *I* is your real being; that *I* is the divinity of your being. *I* is the one, infinite, eternal Ego; *I* is that which the Master revealed in his statement, "I am the way, the truth, and the life." [7] *I* is the bread, the wine, and the water. *I! I* is not body; *I* is not limitation; *I* is not confined in a body; *I* is. Moses revealed, "I AM THAT I AM," [8] and the Master revealed that same great truth.

Why then are you seeking? What could be more ridiculous than that you, who are one with the Father, and upon whom the Father has bestowed all that He has through heirship, should be seeking for health, wealth, security, or peace? Rather than seeking, would it not be better to leave your "nets," become still, and realize:

I already am! I already am living in divine Consciousness; I already am in the Father's house. The Father's house is my home; the Father's kingdom is my kingdom. As the Divine Son, I wear the royal robe of divine sonship and the jeweled ring of authority, of dominion over all that is.

Shall I seek for good like a beggar when I am joint-heir with Christ to all there is? No, my roaming and wandering have come to an end. No more to search, no more to seek, no more to roam, no more to wander! Only to be home in Thee!

Thank You, Father. Thank You, Father. All that You have is mine. All that You are, I am. I am home in You.

[7] John 14:6.   [8] Exodus 3:14.

Should you now seek love from anyone, gratitude, or co-operation? Or should you give these, express them, let them flow forth from you? Now you have received a new name: Divine Son. Now you live in a New Dimension in which you find yourself fulfilled with all that the Father has. But this new name is just a re-establishment of your true identity because this has always been your name. Originally you were of your Father's house.

The Adam-dream, human existence, began only when a sense of separation arose, a sense of separate "I"-ness, an "I" who had to earn a living, an "I" who had to be self-supporting, an "I" who had to go out and do for itself. When that false sense of "I" sprang up, that is when the prodigal existence began. This name, Divine Son, is not a new name for you. It is your real identity, and now your real relationship to God is being disclosed to you again: once again, after the many, many, many times it has been revealed and lost.

If you have ears that hear and eyes that see, you will find the revelation of your divine sonship in The Infinite Way. You will read there how God reveals Itself and how the Christ reveals Itself as *I AM*. But only in the secret place of your being can you realize your divine sonship. Then when those around you see this Robe and Ring on you, they will know that you have something.

But how will they see this Robe on you and this Ring, since no one is going to vest you with a visible robe and ring? Only because you know your true identity, because you have broken down the barriers that separate you from your divine sonship. That Robe and Ring will be visible in the manner of your walking, in the smile on your face, in the way in which you live, in your so very evident lack of concern for tomorrow and tomorrow's manna, tomorrow's safety or tomorrow's security.

Those who live and move and have their being in "the secret place of the most High" [9] have no concern about tomorrow's manna, safety, security, happiness, or freedom. No, they have the hidden manna. They have that inner peace that no man can take from them, that inner peace that makes for all outer harmonies.

No man can take from you your God-given peace, just as no man can take from you your God-given freedom. If you attain your spiritual freedom, not even a dictator can take it away from you. If, however, you receive your freedom merely because it is a part of a document called the Constitution of the United States or the Bill of Rights, never forget that just as man wrote that document, so man can annul it. True, you may fight for it, work and strive for it in the external realm; and you may get physical freedom, economic and political freedom, keep them for a while, and then lose them again. But if you realize freedom as part of your being by right of divine sonship, then no man can take from you any part of your kingdom. Your kingdom includes your economic and political security, your physical and your mental health, and your human sense of life, which are but an outer expression of the spiritual. So if you attain your freedom in Christ, no man can violate your Christhood.

My peace *I* give you; *My* freedom *I* give you; *My* health *I* give you; *My* wealth *I* give you; *My* meat, *My* wine, *My* water. How? By acceptance! Live in the consciousness of having all good. "What things soever ye desire, when ye pray, believe that ye receive them." [10] But you say, "How can I believe that I already have when there is no evidence of it?" You cannot, in the external; but you can, once you realize that your divinity repre-

[9] Psalm 91:1.   [10] Mark 11:24.

sents your heirship to all that the Father has. Then you can say, "Oh, yes! All that God has is mine. I have received it by right of inheritance," and whether or not it is visible at this moment on the outer plane is of no importance.

It may well be that tomorrow there may be an appearance contrary to the truth that you are one with the Father. Tomorrow you may be faced with pain, unhappiness, or some form of lack or limitation. Then is the time to bring back to conscious remembrance, "I cannot accept appearances. I cannot judge by appearances. I and the Father are one. That is what I have learned about my true identity, and I stand on, and in, that truth. 'I and my Father are one' [11]—and all that the Father has is mine. I hold to that and maintain it until the outer picture conforms to the inner awareness."

[11] John 10:30.

SEVEN

Grace

————— ‹•› —————

My grace is sufficient for thee.

II Corinthians 12:9

Included in the word "Grace" is all that is meant by the word "gift." The gift of God is a sufficiency. The nations of the world seek after what they shall eat, what they shall drink, wherewithal they shall be clothed. They are continuously taking thought or being concerned about their affairs of tomorrow. This is not true in "My kingdom," which is not of this world. In the kingdom of Grace, God is the creative principle, the infinite power. The word "Grace" implies that which maintains and sustains: infinite good, and above all, love. Therefore, love must be the measure of the capacity of our good.

Grace is fulfillment, and Grace does not bring partial success or partial happiness, nor does it demand of us that which we cannot fulfill. Grace brings a task to us, but with it, Grace brings the understanding, the strength, and the wisdom to perform it; and Grace also brings whatever is necessary for its fulfillment, whether transportation, funds, books, teachers, or teachings.

Under Grace, tomorrow is not our concern, but God's; and whatever is given us to do must be done to the highest of our present understanding. It makes no difference whether it is shopping, selling, teaching, or healing, God has placed that responsibility upon us. God has given us that task, that joy, that privilege, and we execute it to the best of our ability, and then, if necessary, wait expectantly for the next task to be given to us. To doubt that it will be given, to doubt that it will carry with it all the strength and resources necessary to carry it to fruition, to doubt that it will bring with it joy and success is to have no understanding of the meaning of Grace.

Everything that comes by Grace comes as fulfillment, so there is never an occasion to say, "Oh, Father, You have provided a good job for me in New York, but what about the fare to reach there?" Or, "Father, You have provided an inspirational and uplifting class for me to attend, but nobody to leave at home with the family." No, that never happens! Whatever comes by Grace comes as fulfillment.

The ravens are fed, and the lilies are clothed through Grace —not through man. Man can be the instrument, but man cannot grow a garden. God does that. God, acting and appearing as man, is the avenue or instrument through which the necessary work is done.

If you called upon a spiritual teacher for help, would you not be greatly surprised if that teacher said, "Don't you see what a wonderful teacher I am?" You would be shocked at that, because you know that the teacher is but an avenue for God's grace. As a matter of fact, if that teacher were not there and you were seeking your good through God, another teacher would be provided; and if there were none left on earth, whatever was necessary for your spiritual unfoldment would come to you directly from within your own being. However, as long as an instrument, an avenue, or a channel is necessary, if you keep looking to God, divine Grace, for your good, God will raise up whoever is necessary for you. Yes, even in the wilderness, God will raise up a spiritual teacher for you. God has mysterious ways of bringing your good to you when you look to Him, and to Him alone.

Some years ago in a city on the West Coast, a man came to me in regard to a business matter, and in the course of the conversation asked about the nature of my work. It is not easy to explain this to a person who has no knowledge of mysticism,[1] but I told him that it was a teaching, a way of life.

"Oh, a way of life. Well, how is it that I haven't heard of your being in town?"

"Probably because we do not advertise."

"But I have been seeking just that, a way of life. I am not satisfied with the way things are, and I am seeking something else, but I don't know where to look, or how, and here you are in town with what may be the answer, and how do people know you are here?"

[1] The message of The Infinite Way is a purely mystical one even though metaphysical principles are used in the practical application of its teachings. The Infinite Way accepts the definition of the word "mysticism" as given in Merriam-Webster's *Unabridged Dictionary,* Third International Edition, as follows: "the experience of mystical union or direct communion with ultimate reality reported by mystics . . . a theory of mystical knowledge; the doctrine or belief that direct knowledge of God, of spiritual truth, of ultimate reality, or comparable matters is attainable through immediate intuition, insight, or illumination and in a way differing from ordinary sense perception."

"Well," I replied, "when the need is there, they find us."

"But how could I have found you?"

And I said, "You have."

Do you see? There was no advertising on our part, and yet it brought him; and he was not searching for The Infinite Way or for me. He was seeking a way of life; but in seeking a way of life, without thinking of an avenue, he was led to an avenue. It may prove to have been the very one he wanted and needed, but even if it does not, no harm has been done because it will set him on the path that will ultimately lead him to his way. He did not have to pray for a thing; he did not have to pray for a person: all he had to do was to lift himself to the desire for a way, for good, and then he found it. As long as you are not seeking person, place, or thing, as long as your desire is to be fed spiritually, the realization of divine Grace will interpret itself on your level of understanding.

To me, divine Grace is the realization that God meets the needs of His children, and therefore it is not necessary to go out and proselyte in an attempt to force them to a realization of that Grace. God knows the needs of His children, and when His children are ready for a spiritual teaching He will lead them to the particular teaching necessary for their unfoldment. Let each follow the light as it is given to him of God, and then he will live by Grace. God brings to all those in the world the unfoldment necessary for their demonstration, and to me, that is another phase of Grace.

It is divine Grace if you can feel that whatever the task given to you, the presence of God is there to fulfill it with you or for you. It is divine Grace to go about your work knowing, not that you have to do it, but that you are the instrument through which it is done.

Grace is the realization that you can perform every task allotted to you. You can execute every duty given to you. You can carry through with any work and every work because the responsibility is not yours. The idea is God's; the wisdom is God's; the strength is God's; the necessary love, substance, and activity are God's. And that, too, is divine Grace.

It is divine Grace that you are enabled to fulfill every demand upon you, and this Grace leaves you free and joyous to experience what is called this human life; but this life, understood through Grace, is not a human life at all: it is really divine.

Grace also includes forgiveness. Sometimes we hold ourselves in bondage to the belief of deserved punishment for sins of omission or commission, and often we hold others in bondage to these same beliefs. But under this life of Grace, there is forgiveness without any consideration for whether one has deserved, earned, or been worthy of it. The forgiveness is there because Grace reveals that the transgressor has not done this thing to you: he has done it unto himself, through ignorance.

"Father, forgive them; for they know not what they do." [2] You might think that the Master meant that they knew not what they did to him. He did not mean that at all. He meant that they did not know what they were doing to themselves. To him, nothing could happen. He had come under divine sonship. God was his eternal life, and no one could take that from him. God was his supply: he had already demonstrated that he could feed the multitudes. No one could take that power and ability away from him. He knew that they could do nothing to him; and the only possible meaning of "Father, forgive them" was that they did not know what they were doing to themselves.

The true sense of forgiveness is a realization that no one can harm you. All anyone can do is do something, but he does it to

[2] Luke 23:34.

himself—not to you. Why? Having accepted God as your being, what can happen to you? Can you be deprived of life, health, liberty, freedom, or supply? No! No! No one can take your supply from you because it does not come from man: it comes from God. No one can deprive you of anything; no one can harm you. You and your Father are one. Can anyone break that relationship? No! Then no one can do anything to you, and so when you say, "Father, forgive them," you are really saying that they do not know what they are doing to themselves in accepting the belief in a selfhood apart from God, in accepting into their consciousness hate, envy, jealousy, fear, or malice.

No one can be brought to harm who understands his divine sonship, who has recognized his life through Grace, the gift of God. Anyone who recognizes God to be a sanctuary, his abiding place, can never come under the injuries wrought by wars, bombs, or accidents.

It is only in your sense of separation from God that such things can happen. Neither height nor depth—being up in an airplane or being down in a submarine—can separate you from the life of God or from the love of God. Love means care; love means protection; love means security; and love means safety. So what difference would it make, up or down? What difference would it make, bombs or no bombs? Is there any peril or sword that could separate you from the love of God? Yes, there is! Yes, there is! Your acceptance of a sense of separation from God will do it! Your sense of having a life of your own that can begin and end will do it! Your sense of gaining something at somebody else's expense will do it! Your belief that destroying some other nation will enrich yours or make your nation secure will do it!

Those who thought they could benefit by the destruction of the Germans and Germany lived to find out that it was a very short and not a very sweet victory; and those who later felt that they were going to benefit by the destruction of Hitler and the Nazis, of Japan, or of Russia must have learned that safety and security can never be found in another's destruction. Safety and security can be found in only one way: through Grace.

Grace is love, and love worketh no injury to any man. But you must bring yourself in love to a dependence on the gift of the grace of God, not on the power of the sword or bombs, or on the power of unfair competition.

When you turn to a spiritual unfoldment, you learn one thing: there is no way of getting anything from anyone; there is no way of getting anything out of anything; and there is no hope for those who expect to *get*. Life, spiritually understood, is not a getting process: it is a giving process. You will get out of life whatever you put into it, no more and no less. It may be a life of peace, but there will be no peace or prosperity for those who are expecting to get something. It may be a life of war and depression, but there will be no war or depression to the person who is putting into life his love, his forgiveness, and his dependence on Grace. To that person, none of these things will come nigh his dwelling place.

If you could learn the secret of Grace, which is a complete reliance on this infinite Power within, you would find a spiritual freedom in the outer realm that no man could take from you. Under a life of Grace, there would come a total freedom from the capacity to injure or to be injured. Divine Grace would reveal to you your divine sonship, and that same Grace would maintain and sustain that divine sonship under any and all circumstances.

EIGHT

Living the Life of Grace

———————◄•►———————

God is infinite, and God manifests Itself in infinite forms and in infinite ways. God is consciousness, and we therefore become aware of all those things necessary to our unfoldment through an activity of consciousness. We see, hear, taste, touch, and smell, but these are all activities of consciousness manifested at different levels.

Often in meditation it is possible to see visions or to hear the still small voice; and then there are times when the Presence makes itself known through the activity of smell, and even of touch. We may feel a touch on the shoulder, the head, or on the cheek. At other times, the fragrance of flowers may be noticed. There is no way to limit God and feel that He can appear in one way only. God can appear in any form, and probably we can understand that best by recalling that when Joan of Arc was asked, "Does God speak to you in French?" her reply was, "I do not know in what language God speaks, but I hear Him in French."

Does God speak as perfume or odors, voices, or a touch? No! But we can comprehend God in these ways. That is our interpretation of God's presence. Let us learn to accept God in whatever way and in whatever form God may appear to us. How do we know that it is God? How do we know that it is not imagination? By the fruitage, by the results.

When we are indulging in vain imaginings about our spiritual activities and spiritual work, it leaves us up in the air, dangling in space, with no tangible results. But when our experience is actually an experience of God, we can know it by its fruits, and the fruits of the Spirit are joy, peace, prosperity, health, harmony, and love. When the Presence announces Itself, there comes with It a sense of serenity, tranquility, a peace which may translate itself into form.

Everything has form: even thought. All substance must have a form although not a form always visible to our human sense, and the higher we go in spiritual realization and unfoldment, the more we see the spiritual sense of form rather than its material sense, and the more aware we are of spiritual reality. For example, a person with a purely material sense of life looks out and sees faces and figures, hats, dresses, suits, eyeglasses, and earphones. But as he rises higher and higher, he becomes less aware of these things and more aware of a look in the eye, a smile on the lips, a flick of the finger. He becomes less conscious of men and women as such, and more aware of those outer symbols that express inward being. Then there comes a state when he continues to rise above even that, and he is almost unaware of people as human beings. At that stage, he senses or realizes the spiritual nature of their being.

Our entire existence represents states and stages of consciousness. In one state of consciousness, we do things one way, but as we evolve or develop spiritually into another state of consciousness, we do them in another way. For example, until we learn that God's grace is sufficient for us, we think that we have to labor, to plot and plan for our future. We worry, fear, and doubt. Perhaps we have all kinds of human anxieties and thoughts and fears about ourselves and our families and our future; and here an idea is presented to us that God's grace is sufficient for us. We stop short and wonder, "Is that true? Does that really mean what it says? Does it really mean that God's grace is enough without my doing all this worrying, planning, thinking, and scheming? Is that really true? Have I been wasting time and energy in useless thought-taking when all the time there is a divine Grace at hand that can provide for my sufficiency?"

After you have done some thinking about this, you finally come to the conclusion that you will have to prove it for yourself. Your problems are still with you, probably more than yesterday, but with each one, you bring to conscious remembrance this truth: "Thy grace is sufficient for me. I had better stop worrying and being anxious for a while. I will put off taking thought for today. Right now, I rest in the truth that God's grace is sufficient for me."

So you relax, you rest, and you feel at peace, but that does not mean that tonight, tomorrow, or the day after, you are not going to have more anxious moments, more concern, more lack, more fear, or more pain. Then again you remind yourself that God's grace is sufficient, that you must rest in that Grace with no anxiety, fear, doubt, or thought. You may go along that way for months—three, four, five, or six—and all this time you are meeting every appearance of discord with the remembrance that God's grace is sufficient, even though the outward appearance would deny it.

Just a few days, weeks, or months later, and lo and behold, you may begin to feel God's grace coming into expression in your experience. You find good coming to you that you had not humanly planned for; you find harmony and health coming to you that at the moment you may not be able to explain; but with the passage of time, it dawns in your consciousness, "Why, it is true! God's grace *is* sufficient for me." By that time, you have come to a place where you rest more in that sense of peace and no longer need to use as many statements of truth.

Ah, but then perhaps there comes another problem. This time it may be a great responsibility, and you have the feeling that it is beyond your means, your strength, your time, or perhaps your power to cope with it. Along with that comes the remembrance of a passage of Scripture, and you hear: "He performeth the thing that is appointed for me." [1]

That startles you for a minute. "What? What? He performeth?" You think you have been given this job or this work to do, or you have been given this responsibility, and yet Scripture says that He performeth it. There again, while you go about the performance of your tasks, you are reminded, "Very well, I can do it because actually He is performing it through me." Again that responsibility drops away. That rest comes, and soon you find that it is true: there is a *He* at the center of your being. He that is within you is greater than any responsibility, duty, or demand that can come upon you from the world.

So while at first you may have been diligent in the use of statements of truth and may have brought them to your awareness

[1] Job 23:14.

over and over and over again, now you find that only occasionally do you have to remind yourself of them because now the
words have given way to the actual awareness itself, and when
you have the awareness, you do not need the words.

This bringing of statements of truth to conscious remembrance
is called contemplative meditation. When you undertake this
form of meditation, you may at first be bringing to conscious remembrance every statement of truth you know. It may take you
a half hour to complete your part of this contemplative part of
the meditation, that is, your voicing of the truth. Then you sit
back and listen, and that part of the meditation may be one minute, two, three, or five. As you continue this form of contemplative meditation, however, you will gradually get to the place
where your part of it takes only five minutes, and God's part
takes a half hour. It just reverses itself. God keeps filling you
with His truth; God keeps filling you with the realization of His
presence; but you have made way for the Spirit by your prepara-
tion through your contemplative meditation. Therefore, do not
hesitate to bring to your conscious remembrance every statement
of truth you know until you have built your consciousness to
where that is no longer necessary.

You do not discard: you just evolve. You grow gradually
from one form of meditation to another, and from one state of
consciousness to another, and in time, you come to the place
where it is only occasionally that it seems necessary consciously
to remember some truth. For the most part, truth is imparting
itself to you from the infinity of your being, sometimes in the
form of quotations that you already know, and very often in a
form that you never heard of before.

Eventually you learn what it means to pray without ceasing.
When that time comes, whenever you hear a news broadcast, see
a headline, or somebody brings you bad news, automatically you

just turn it off with the reminder that in God's kingdom harmony alone reigns. Wherever you may be—on the street, in a bus, in your office, or in your home—when you witness sin, disease, lack, limitation, or death, you automatically realize, "No, that can exist only as a picture in the human mind, not as any part of God's kingdom. God's kingdom could never hold any such pictures as that." And so you are praying without ceasing, and yet you are doing it without consciously going around declaring truth, except as the pictures of sense touch you, and you automatically learn to re-interpret them into their spiritual values.

It is possible to reach the heights attained by Jesus when, without his even knowing that she was there, the woman who pressed through the throng and touched the hem of his robe was healed. Jesus was living in such a high state of spiritual consciousness that he was not even aware of a sick woman near him. Because of his years of training, he was able to lift himself into that exalted state so that without any conscious thought, he did not see any error to deny. When you arrive at the state of consciousness where you never see, hear, taste, touch, or smell any form of error, you are then in a state of consciousness where your meditations and your prayers are wordless, but you can be assured that then you will be meditating and praying all the time.

The one infinite divine Consciousness, called God, is your individual consciousness; and while there are no degrees to It, there are degrees of your awareness of It. That is because of the word "I." When the word "I" was used to identify a human being, that was when a mind apart from God was set up, and that is the experience of the Prodigal.

When I say, "I, Joel," I am referring to a certain state of consciousness. True, it is God-consciousness, but it is limited by my concept of what Consciousness is. If I accept the human view that my consciousness is made up of my prenatal experience, my environment, education, and personal experience, and then think of that as my consciousness, it would be a very limited sense of consciousness, one which would limit me forever. And always, throughout my life, I would have to move in the groove of that consciousness. That is the way of the human world. It says that if you had a certain prenatal experience, a particular kind of environment, education or lack of it, and certain personal experiences, you will move in a foreordained groove. For the most part, people do just that until in some way or other spiritual wisdom is brought to them in some fashion, and the revelation given that that is all foolishness.

The truth is that God is the measure of your consciousness. God is the circle and the circumference of your consciousness, and nothing less than the allness of God belongs to you.

With that point of view, your life begins to change. Instead of looking back and attributing your present situation in life to a lack of education, an unhappy childhood, a discordant family life, or to the unpleasant fact that your grandmother was a neurotic or your grandfather an alcoholic, and so on and on, now, all of a sudden, you come to the realization: "Wait a minute! Wait a minute! What has that to do with me? I am the offspring of God, and God is my parent, God is my inheritance, God is my environment. I am not limited to that personal sense of consciousness, or to a subconscious or superconsciousness. I am limited only to whatever limitations there are upon God, and since God is infinite there are none."

Now you begin to live out from a new basis. You are living out from the universal Consciousness which is pouring Itself into you, and you are letting It come into you and pour forth through you. If you do that, what becomes of the inhibitions you believed arose out of your childhood, your education or lack of it, or your wealth or lack of it? All that would be broken down instantly, and your prayer becomes, "Flow, God; flow! Flow into me and through me, and out into this vast world."

This would reveal to you the true meaning of humility. You would know then that you not only have no limitations, but that you can take no praise for your accomplishments, since it is all God pouring Itself through. Then you will really know in all humility that there is absolutely no limitation upon your being.

You are Self-complete through God: not Self-complete because of your education, not Self-complete because you have inherited a fortune, not Self-complete because of some human circumstance or condition; but Self-complete because God is your life, your soul, and your consciousness. With God as the infinite nature of your being, what becomes of limitation? There is none. It all disappears.

The nature of the entire message of The Infinite Way is the revelation of God as individual identity and capacity, God as infinite being, and God as the infinity of individual being. The essence of the entire Message is: "I can of mine own self do nothing.[2] . . . The Father that dwelleth in me, he doeth the works." [3] What work? Limited work? No, infinite work! Infinite because of you or me? No, infinite because of the infinity of God.

Do you not see that until you wipe out all that sense of limitation that has come about by believing that you are limited to a finite mind, a subconscious mind, a superconscious mind, or any other kind of mind, and realize that there is only one mind, and that it is the instrument of God, and it is infinite, you will always be limited. God is the only capacity you have, and therefore, there is no limit to your capacity. Think; pray; meditate on God

[2] John 5:30.   [3] John 14:10.

as your intelligence, God as your life, God as the measure of your capacity, God as the infinite nature of your being!

How can you be immortal or eternal? *You* cannot be, except as God is immortal and eternal. There is only one immortality, and the immortality of God is the immortality of your being. How can you be loving? *You* cannot: only God is love. But the measure of your love is the measure of God since God is love. To think that you have it in your power to be loving, in and of yourself, or that you have it within your power to be generous, kind, or just would be to believe that you had gone beyond the demonstration of Jesus Christ. It may happen some day, but it has not happened yet. Remember, Jesus himself said, "Why callest thou me good? there is none good but one, that is, God." [4]

So with us. When you learn that love is not a personal quality, you are able not only to love infinitely but to be loved infinitely. It is only when you limit love to your personal capacity for love that you find love very, very limited. It is only when you think of justice as being a quality of this man's character or that man's nature that you find it limited. But when you see that love or justice is of God, there is no limitation to it any more. You have then removed the egotism that would think that you can be loving, even though Jesus said that there is none good but one. You cannot be loving, neither can you withhold love because God is love, and God is forever expressing Itself as love to every open avenue. And that you are. There is where the practice must come.

"My grace is sufficient for thee," [5] but it will not come into active expression until that statement of truth passes from being a statement to being an inner conviction:

[4] Matthew 19:17.　　　[5] II Corinthians 12:9.

Thy grace is sufficient for me. Thy law is sufficient for me, and I will have no dealings with any other sense of law—only the spiritual. Thy strength is sufficient for me. It is not a question of the strength of my muscles; it is not a question of my strength: Thy strength is sufficient for me. Thy love is sufficient for me.

As you come into the awareness that God's love is sufficient for you, God's love is made evident to you through men and women. "If a man say, I love God, and hateth his brother, he is a liar: for he that loveth not his brother whom he hath seen, how can he love God whom he hath not seen?" [6] In other words, then, by first looking away from men and women, and realizing that the only love that can come to you is the love of God, more than likely it will appear as, or through, men and women and children and the world at large: as animals, birds, and plants. It will come to you through God, as God's love expressed as some measure of form.

God's wisdom, too, is sufficient for you. Is there any need, then, for being concerned about your wisdom or mine, or our lack of wisdom? No, you are opening yourself now to God's wisdom that is sufficient for you. And God's wisdom fills you. God's love fills you. God's presence is sufficient for you. God's presence! And you may have been thinking in terms of husband, wife, sister, brother, friend, or other relatives, but here you are faced with the truth that God's presence is sufficient for you. Just think of that: God's presence.

Most persons do not believe that. As a rule, they do not accept it. They talk in terms of God's presence, and then turn around and cry their hearts out for some other presence—some-

[6] I John 4:20.

times even for the absence of some other presence. But the real truth is that God's presence is sufficient for them, and as they rest back in that conviction, God's presence appears to them as the presence of friends, relatives, husband, wife, child, whoever it may be.

Carry this with you; practice it today, and practice it tonight; practice it tomorrow morning, so that you will be able to have the experience of God's grace unfolding, unfolding, and unfolding.

NINE

The New Dimension

————◄●►————

The human scene continues to unfold day by day, as it has throughout all the days of the past. There is always the temptation to hope that things will be different tomorrow. But left to itself, one day will follow another as days always have. The human scene is a state of inertia; it continues being whatever it is now, usually along the same lines. Nothing will be different tomorrow from what it is today, or from what it has been in the past until a new note is brought into the picture.

"Strait is the gate, and narrow is the way, which leadeth unto life, and few there be that find it.[1] . . . I came not to send

[1] Matthew 7:14.

peace, but a sword." [2] Up to now, what has been said is gentle and sweet, and good-tasting. Now comes the part that makes the "belly bitter": [3] the living of this truth. This demands sacrifice and great effort.

It will not be too difficult for you to remember the truth that you and the Father are one and all that the Father has is yours: the difficulty comes in living it, and it is only in the living of it that it can be demonstrated. Declaring, "I and my Father are one," [4] or declaring your sonship will be of little help to you. You must assume your obligation as a Son. Part of the responsibility entailed in that relationship lies in your readiness and willingness to leave your "nets" in the sense of stopping your search for health and supply and to rest in the conscious awareness of these as divine gifts already established within your being, even though momentarily not visible outwardly. This means no longer voicing truth, but living the truth of your identity, being willing to be called upon to heal or feed the multitudes. Can you do it? You can, if you realize, "I of my own self cannot do it, but by virtue of my divine sonship, I can. All that the Father has is mine: the gift of healing, the infinity of supply, the joy of sharing and the joy of giving, the wisdom of not bearing resentment, anger, malice, and jealousy."

That is the living of this truth, living so that when the world hurls hurts at you, you do not give in and react to the hurt, but rather realize, "In my divine sonship, there can be no hurt, and whatever it is that this old mortal selfhood feels cannot disturb me now. That was the Prodigal out there on the road, and I have left him out there. Whatever is aimed at the Prodigal is of no concern to me. Whatever is aimed at my Christhood, the Christ

[2] Matthew 10:34.   [3] Revelation 10:9.   [4] John 10:30.

can absorb, just as the Christhood of Jesus absorbed the nails and the pain of the Crucifixion and brought him to the Resurrection."

The personal identity of Jesus did not bring this about. His body could not, but his Christhood could take everything that was leveled at him, and then he could walk out of the tomb. It was Jesus' Christhood that enabled him to do that. So with you, too, it is not your humanhood, it is not your prodigal sonship, and certainly not your human selfhood that can withstand trials and tribulations or that has any hidden manna to give. It is out of your Christhood that you can heal and feed multitudes and forgive seventy times seven.

Do you not know that as a human being you cannot help resenting injuries and that you cannot hold these human emotions of envy, jealousy, and malice in check? Each person is touched by some hurt: resentment, pique, anger, or frustration. You cannot help that in your humanhood, but the Christhood of your being can accept and dissolve it, if only you omit the word "I." Omit the word "I": "I cannot be hurt. That was not aimed at me; that is no part of my being, so let the Christhood of me absorb it."

Do you not know that if Jesus had not lived his Christhood on the Cross, those nails would have killed him? Physicality cannot withstand such an experience, but Christhood can.

All the human wisdom you can gain will not heal anyone or feed anyone, nor will it give you the priceless hidden manna to give out to the world. But through your recognition of your sonship, you can say, "Ask me for water, and I will give you water, the water of everlasting life. Come to me with your burdens, and I will give you rest. I will give you peace. I will give you comfort."

Comfort out of what? What you have learned out of a book? No! No! No! Out of your Divinity, out of your Christhood, out of the hidden manna that is given to you as a child of God, out of the meat that the world knows not of, that meat that you carry around with you. That meat, you can give to the world to eat of; that bread, wine, and water you can give, not out of your storehouse, but out of your Christhood.

This is easy to put into words, but it is not easy to put into practice. It is not easy to acknowledge, every moment of every day, your divine sonship, the New Dimension, so that when called upon, you do not respond with "I haven't any money to give you," but rather with "Yes, I have hidden manna to share with you. I have meat that the world knows not of. I have living waters to give you."

Out of your Christhood, you can solve any problem that comes to you. You, of yourself, cannot give human comfort. This is a word of wisdom to all those who are now, or who at some time may be, called upon for spiritual help. But always remember it matters not one whit what your past experience may have been: it is not sufficient to warrant you in advising anybody about his personal affairs. So, when anyone comes to you with problems concerning his home life, his business or social life, be very careful that you say nothing except "Now let us meditate, and bring the Christ to bear on the situation."

Your faith and reliance are always on the inner Grace, the hidden manna, the meat that the world knows not of, the inner living waters, not on visible wisdom. The Christ of you, the Spirit of the Father in you, is a "peace, be still" to error of every nature. The Christhood of you is a "peace, be still" to every storm, but do not try to be so omnipotently wise that you give advice. It may be good advice, but it will backfire some day. Do not do it! You bring to bear your divine sonship, and out of the hidden manna those who come to you for help will be directed, led, protected, and sustained. Remain steadfast in your Christhood; bring the Christ to bear on any and every situation.

You need have no hesitancy in approaching any problem for anyone, no matter how great it may be. It may have to do with national or international affairs; it may have to do with state or community affairs. What matter? Do not hesitate. There is nothing too big for you to deal with through your hidden manna, which is the Christhood of your being. But be sure you are dealing with it through your Christhood, not your humanhood.

Miracles will happen through the Christ of your being, but only trouble will come through giving human advice and human guidance. Never, never give advice!

Remember, your dimension now is the Christ; your dimension is a "stone . . . cut out of the mountain without hands," [5] the white stone whose name is Christ, the Invisible. As you turn to It, you have no tangible evidence of the help at hand, but you have an inner assurance and realization of a Presence that goes before you. You have an inner awareness of tomorrow's manna, even though you cannot see it today; and you live by that inner Grace.

But have you the right to tell another person that he must live by the standards that you have achieved, probably through years and years of struggle, and strife, and seeking, and searching? Oh, no! Give him of your hidden manna, which is the Christ, and then let the Christ appear to him in the form necessary for his unfoldment. Retire quietly and gently into the center of your being, and there realize the presence of divine Grace, acknowledging that henceforth you live, not by struggle or by strife, but by the Grace of your sonship.

[5] Daniel 2:45.

Your good is yours as a gift of God. Accept it as that. But while you are in the Spirit, you are free—silently, of course—to invite the whole world in to sup with you: "Come, come, all ye that labor and are heavy laden. Come to this spiritual feast. Let me share with you this divine Grace that has come to me as a gift of God. Let me give you of the waters of life from the hidden Spring. Let me give you of this hidden manna, this spiritual food and rest. Let me share with you this inner meat, and let me give you what measure of *My* peace I have found: *My* gentle, gentle peace, the peace that passes understanding, the peace that goes before you to 'make the crooked places straight.' " " [6]

"Let the reign of God be with you, for His kingdom endureth forever. Withdraw your gaze from the outer realm, and in the silence of your being, realize that you are home in God, that no more do you look outside into the prodigal experience for your good."

Do the work the Father gives you to do every moment, whatever its name or nature, knowing that as you do it to the utmost of your present ability, it fits you for more, and always higher, work in His service. You are no longer "man, whose breath is in his nostrils." You have no needs; you have no desires: now you have the realization of fulfillment, since now you know and have discovered *I*.

Now you know what it is that has come that you might be fulfilled: It is the *I* that you found yourself to be when you knew that you were not your body, but that your body was yours. Now you know that that *I* is come that you might be fulfilled.

Henceforth, you draw upon the *I* that you are; henceforth, you draw upon the kingdom of God within you for your good;

[6] Isaiah 45:2.

and even while using the mode and means of the outer world, you acknowledge that your good flows from within.

Perhaps tomorrow you may have to make excuses for not paying a bill. Perhaps tomorrow you may have to admit that you are in pain, but within yourself you will still realize that this divine sonship is your assurance of peace, freedom, power, joy, and dominion. As long as you steadfastly hold to this inner integrity, as long as you live as though you were the Christ, the outer picture will soon begin to conform to your inner awareness, to "the pattern shewed to thee in the mount." [7] This pattern that has been revealed to you in the higher consciousness will be made evident and visible to you when you return to the valley. That which is whispered in your ear will be revealed to all the world.

If you can accept your true identity and live in that awareness, you can welcome the whole world to come to you for comfort, substance, supply, guidance, healing, reformation, Christhood— welcome the entire world, without limitation, knowing that even though you of yourself can do nothing, because of your Christhood, all the gifts of the Father are yours to bestow, without judgment, without price.

Show forth by your demonstration that you have received a new name, Divine Son, joint-heir with Christ in God: no longer "man, whose breath is in his nostrils," no longer "worm of the dust," no longer a beggar seeking health and wealth.

Always listen for the Voice within you, and you will hear It say, "Son . . . all that I have is thine.[8] . . . Fear not: for I am with thee." [9] Only say unto the children of men that they must return to the Father's house. They will not find freedom outside, or peace—not peace of mind or peace of soul or peace

---

[7] Hebrews 8:5.   [8] Luke 15:31.   [9] Isaiah 43:5.

of body. Peace is to be found only in the inner Kingdom by resting in divine sonship.

"The kingdom of God is within you," [10] but do not go around mouthing these words. How many times have I told you in the Writings that God cannot be known, that God must be experienced? Go within. There is a Presence in you; there is a Spirit in you. Learn to abide with It: "Acquaint now thyself with him, and be at peace." [11] *I* will give you rest, and peace, and strength. But where will you meet *Me*? Within your own being! And how will you become acquainted with *Me*? Commune within yourself. You must make for yourself minutes and hours of time for communion. You must have union; you must have realization.

Withdraw from the outer world. You do not have to let your wisdom be known until you have proved it to the fullest, so do not be in a hurry to tell this to anyone. Be quiet! Be quiet! No one is asking you to advertise it; no one is asking you to proselyte; no one is asking you to make it known. Make it your own; make it your own!

Live as though you were the son of God, which you really are. Refute all appearances to the contrary; stand fast in the faith that you have gained. Stand fast in the assurance you have received within your own being that divine sonship is the truth of your identity. Rest from the mental and physical struggle to achieve and to attain, and let the kingdom of God flow forth from you.

"I will never leave thee, nor forsake thee.[12] . . . Whither thou goest, I will go." [13] You cannot get away from *I,* and that *I* has come that you might be fulfilled. "In quietness and in confidence shall be your strength." [14] The assurance that the Lord is your shepherd will be your strength. No longer rest in your

[10] Luke 17:21.   [11] Job 22:21.   [12] Hebrews 13:5.
[13] Ruth 1:16.   [14] Isaiah 30:15.

health or in your wealth, but rest in your assurance of the divine Presence and of your sonship.

How do you know that the health and harmony and wholeness of Being is yours? Only because you know your true identity as Christ, the son of God. "Know ye not that your body is the temple of the Holy Ghost?" [15] Do you not know that the tabernacle of God is with men? The tabernacle, the temple, the body, the business, the health, the harmony, the wholeness of God: all these are with men by right of sonship.

By right of sonship, manna is stored up within you. By right of sonship, the spiritual meat and spiritual water are stored up within you. How much of it? All that the Father has! Come! Come to these waters! Eat and drink! Say that to the world. Invite the world to come to you. Out of your sonship, you can share the manna, the water, the wine, the bread, and the meat.

So now I say to you: You have assumed your new identity, your new-old identity; you have accepted your relationship now as the son of God, and you are acknowledging this identity. At least once each day—if possible, more often—remember to retire into your inner being for the touch of the Christ, for the realization of the Presence. Whether you achieve it at first is not important: the important thing is that you continue in the effort of retiring into your inner being and there making contact with this inner Self, this hidden manna, until you feel the Impulse. Then you will know that whatever the circumstances of your human experience—whether of business, home, health, or wealth —a change will take place, and a change for the better.

It is this inner sense of God's presence, this inner realization of your divinity, that will appear outwardly as the changed condition. Do not look for any change except in proportion as the

[15] I Corinthians 6:19.

activity of the Christ has been realized and felt within. At first, you are perhaps seeking this through, or with, the help of your teacher, and your teacher, achieving this Christ in your behalf, will bring about a change in your outer affairs. But remember that ultimately it will be your responsibility to make this contact for yourself.

The help of a teacher is not a permanent dispensation. " 'If I go not away, the Comforter will not come unto you' [16]—if I keep on feeding and healing you, the Comforter, the realization of the Christ in you, will not come." Why? Because you will be continuously expecting it from outside, from someone else. That does not mean that a student should not reach out to his teacher for help as often as may be necessary to bridge over the period until he himself reaches that Christ-consciousness, and even after that there may be some periods in which he will still require the help of one further along the Path than he.

That is legitimate. But remember this: the change in the outer appearance will come only as the activity or presence of the Christ is realized. So, whether at first it is through your teacher or whether it is ultimately through your own realization, it is the touch of the Christ, and that alone, that will change the picture without.

The Christ is a living presence and power, the greatest power ever known or realized. The Christ in all times, and for all those who have achieved It, has overcome the world, not for the world, but for you and for me who have discovered and felt It. Everyone who has ever achieved Christ has been set free from the trials and tribulations and strife of the world.

Jesus the Christ was free of all discords and inharmonies for himself, and whatever he suffered, he suffered because of his

[16] John 16:7.

work with his followers: his world. So with every master, with every revelator, and with every teacher, there has come enough of the activity and realization of the Christ to set them free forever from the discords and inharmonies of the world, but as they take on the burdens of their world, they also come under a sense at times of the struggle of the world. For themselves in their individual experience, however, they are free.

Your world of tomorrow will be the same as your world of today, except in proportion as a touch of the Christ is realized. Once the Christ is realized and felt in the Kingdom within, It manifests in the outer world in every form necessary to your daily harmony.

TEN

"Inasmuch as Ye Have Done It Unto One of the Least"

———————◄●►———————

To those engaged in spiritual work, there is a certain reward that comes in the feeling of having served their fellow man and of having served God in such service. That is as it should be. When we come to giving service within our family, business, or even community life, however, we are likely to forget that the service we perform for another is not really for another at all. It is not done because we happen to have a husband or a wife or because we are parents, neighbors, or because we are citizens of one nation under one flag.

Outwardly, it would seem that we are performing our duties and obligations merely because of those human obligations and relationships, but this is not true. In serving another, we are in reality serving the Christ. We are serving God. It makes no difference whether it is supporting our family or contributing to some philanthropic enterprise, we are not now doing it as human beings doing it unto human beings: we are doing it unto the Christ of their being. It is the Christ of them calling out to the Christ of us, and we answer that call.

As long as we think that we are merely serving man, feeding, educating, and sustaining our families, or co-operating with our business associates, we are so far missing the mark that we lay ourselves open to betrayal, ingratitude, and all the evils of human nature. Only from the moment that we begin to understand that any service that we give to our fellow man is in reality our devotion to God made manifest, only then are we serving in the manner of the Christ, and only then will we reap the spiritual reward or fruitage of our service and our devotion.

The moment that anyone serves us as human beings, the gratitude, appreciation, or reward he receives is in proportion to our capacity to give it. We may be able one day to give a great deal to one, and none at all on another day to someone else. However, when a person who performs any service for us whatsoever, even to the delivery of our groceries, realizes that he is not doing it as a service to man, but as a devotion to the God in man or to the God who appears as man, we shall find that there is no way under the sun that we can respond to that individual except in love, with gratitude and appreciation.

The mistakes that we have made is that we have served man, separate and apart from our service to God, instead of realizing that our service to man represents our devotion to God, since "If a man say, I love God, and hateth his brother, he is a liar." [1] Why? Because there is no God separate and apart from man, and

[1] I John 4:20.

the only devotion we can ever pay to God is in our devotion to man.

It is not necessary to voice this to anyone. On the contrary, it is another one of those secret wisdoms to be held close within ourselves. Whatever service we perform, regardless of for whom we perform it, we realize, "Friend, I am not doing this for you. I am not too much interested in you as you, but this act represents my devotion to God appearing as you. This represents my devotion to the divine Selfhood of you, and so I perform this service lovingly, willingly, and generously, knowing that it is my recognition of God and His kingdom on earth."

There is no kingdom of heaven except on earth, so there is no way to achieve heaven except through achieving it on earth; and the only way to achieve heaven on earth is to serve God on earth, and the only way to serve God on earth is to serve man in the realization of God as man's real being.

A miracle takes place when we stop being human do-gooders, when we stop merely serving man on the level of man and begin to realize, "Why, I would serve you if you were not you, since you are God manifest. I would serve you if I had never met you. I would give you the same time, the same effort, the same joy, the same sharing, whether I knew you personally or not. Why? Because this sharing represents my devotion to God manifest as the Son."

So it is, we could never give of our time, effort, service, or money to God without finding that there were twelve baskets full left over. Only if we thought that we were giving out of our personal selfhood and giving it to some other personal selfhood, who might or might not be worthy or deserving of it—only then would we find that in giving we were depleting ourselves. In that case, if we gave money, we would have less left; if we gave service, we would have less time for ourselves; but the moment that we have the Christ-approach—"I can of my own self do nothing. I have no possessions. All that the Father has is mine, but it always remains the Father's, and so whatever I share is of the Father"—we can give away the whole kingdom of the Father, and we will still have more than enough to care for our needs. Only when we think of it as of our own are we depleting ourselves.

This is true also of strength, and of our hours of devotion or service. The moment we think of them as ours, we will soon find how limited and finite they are, and how little good they accomplish. But when we see that we are giving of our personal strength or service, realizing that it is not ours at all, and that we are giving even of our hours during the day out of the infinite storehouse of God's hours, we will find that we have more than a sufficiency.

Think of a mother who gives and gives and gives to her children, and is not depleted, tired, wearied, or worn. This is possible only as long as the animating principle is love. The love that produced one or twelve children produces an infinity of supply to take care of them and, in addition, the time, effort, and energy necessary to provide for their needs. On the other hand, every sense of loss, lack, or depletion, every sense of frustration, ingratitude, or misunderstanding represents a lack of wisdom in serving man instead of serving God as man, instead of a devotion to the Christ of man.

In this work, you must have seen over and over again that a teacher who is truly dedicated does not count how many hours of service he may give to you, how many days, or how much effort is required to write to you or give you the necessary help. It does not make any difference whether you have ever met him or not, or whether he is a total stranger to you. It certainly matters not to him whether or not he is going to be paid by you. He is going to be paid, and he knows that. True, it may not be by you, but he knows right well that his devotion to God will never leave him without at least twelve baskets full left over, and oftentimes twelve times twelve.

But does the teacher weigh out his time or effort with you by hours or minutes? No! Because in his spiritual vision he knows that his service or giving is not of himself, but of God, and so he has the whole infinity to give, and he knows that he is not doing it for "man, whose breath is in his nostrils," because that man would never ask for spiritual help. No, it takes a person of spiritual insight to ask for spiritual help and to appreciate it. So the spiritual teacher is never serving man: he is always serving God.

In the Fourth Dimension we are drawing our good, not from out of this world, but from out of the depths of our being. Above all, let me remind you again that this is our basic premise, insofar as it concerns our individual demonstration of Christhood. To his sense of things, a human being derives his good from the world; and so, when seeking any good, thought naturally turns to some person, place, or thing, some business activity, or some outer form of expression. That seems to be natural and the only right thing for the human being to do.

Entering this New Dimension of life, that is, the Christ-life, we never think of drawing our good from the outer realm or from another person; we never think of deriving our good from some outer experience or expression. Through it, yes, but not from it.

So the first and vital work of those living in the Fourth Dimension is meditation. Whether we undertake to heal someone, teach a class, or to engage in selling, housework, farm work, or a business activity—whatever the nature of our work—if we expect success in it on the outer plane, we are the man of earth. But if we know that the outer expression is merely going to be the reflection of the inner, then before undertaking any work, we will turn within.

In turning within, we may bring to our conscious remembrance some scriptural or mystical statement with which we are familiar, such as "Except the Lord build the house, they labour in vain that build it." [2] This is acknowledging that whether we are performing a family, business, or civic duty, unless God prospers it, there is no real assurance of success. But since the kingdom of God is within, there is the necessity for contacting God in order to be sure that God is building our house. Our first obligation in meditation, then, is for the purpose of establishing that God-contact. Or we may bring to remembrance: "He performeth the thing that is appointed for me.[3] . . . The Lord will perfect that which concerneth me." [4] In knowing that, we have placed the responsibility where it belongs, on His shoulders, on the shoulders of this Infinite Invisible, this Christ of our being.

"In all thy ways acknowledge Him." [5] Undertake nothing without acknowledging Him as the Presence, the Power, the Law, the Cause, and the Effect. In doing this over and over and over again—never from the standpoint of a formula or a repetition of statements, but always spontaneously—there develops a state of consciousness which later eliminates much of the time of your meditation work, since it now becomes automatic to realize that only the Father can perform this, and that you of your own self can do nothing. In this realization, in the making of this contact, comes forth the spiritual fruitage in your life. Your life, therefore, must be a continual turning within to be fed.

The real values in life are spiritual, not material, and the deep things of God make for a greater peace than any peace that the

2 Psalm 127:1.   3 Job 23:14.
4 Psalm 138:8.   5 Proverbs 3:6.

world can give. There is no good thing that can come into your experience as a permanent dispensation except as it is given to you of the Father. There is no good thing to be achieved permanently on the outer realm, and only as you learn to make that contact with God and maintain it, does your life become the spontaneous outflowing and outpouring of the Spirit.

This even eliminates from your experience any sense of giving service and devotion to your fellow man; it even takes from you a sense of service and devotion to your family as a family. It gives you the complete realization that whether you are doing it for friend, family, or neighbor, you are doing it for the Christ, you are serving only spiritual being. In turn, when you are served, there must come the realization that it is not your vanity that is being glorified, but the Christ of your being that is recognized, served, rewarded, co-operated and shared with.

In this realization, then, the word "I" gradually removes itself; the word "I" becomes of less and less importance until it becomes impossible for that "I" to be hurt, injured, wronged, or defrauded, since all such beliefs would be no part of your being. Even if it seemed to be directed at you, it would be absorbed by the Christ, and responded to by the Christ. So, too, in that realization, you would never be tempted to defraud, wrong, injure, or harm another, or to benefit personally at someone else's expense.

Within you is a deep pool of Spirit, and it is the Source and Fountain of your good. Pray, knock, ask. Only when you pray, when you knock, when you ask, be sure that you are asking and praying only for the Spirit, knocking at the door of Spirit for spiritual unfoldment. Do not attempt to mold Spirit into the human form of companionship, gratitude, or physical improvement. It will interpret Itself on whatever level is necessary, and if the need is for some physical or material thing, the fulfillment will come in that way because "I am come that they might have life, and that they might have it more abundantly." [6] But contact that *Me*, since before *Me* and besides *Me* there is no other God.

Reach into this deep Pool and feel the abundance, the gentleness, and the power of that Spirit, and let It flow; and when It flows, It will come out as in a mold. That mold may be money, home, companions, forgiveness, justice, mercy, kindness, or benevolence; but do not attempt to pour Spirit into a mold, do not attempt to provide a mold in which to hold It.

Go to this Pool, this infinite Pool of joyous substance; commune; feel It as It fills your consciousness, as It circulates within your being. By this I do not mean a physical or an emotional feeling, but an inner awareness of the Divine. That is all! That is seeking the kingdom of God, and then the things are added, because It pours Itself forth, not as ephemeral nothingness or substance, but in molded form, and the mold is always fulfillment.

When supply of whatever name or nature comes out of the depths of *I*, out of the depths of the Soul, when your life is lived in that fourth dimension of the Spirit, there is never just barely enough, and there is never too much. There is bounty, abundance, affluence, but not extravagance, because everything comes as the gift of God, and is meant for your use.

How can you know if you are living in the Fourth Dimension? When your entire vision is on your devotion and service to God, when your expectancy is of God, not of man, but of God, and when you understand that only in His presence is fullness: not in the presence of a person, not in the presence of a bank account. Only in His presence is the fullness of life and the ability to live, move, and have your being in that inner consciousness,

6 John 10:10.

in that inner awareness that "I will never leave thee, nor forsake thee.[7] . . . Whither thou goest, I will go," [8] directing your path, your footsteps, your way.

The whole kingdom of God is within you—the entire kingdom of God in quality and in quantity—and as you discipline yourself to the realization of the great truth that this life, this love, and this abundance must flow out from within you, not come to you, then are you living in the Fourth Dimension, which is the Christ.

But always remember that you block Its flow with every thought of "I," "me," or "mine." You block It with every thought of getting, receiving, or accomplishing. You fulfill It only in the realization that It is flowing forth out of the Godhead, never egotistically from you or from me, never from the sense that you are giving out of your goodness or out of your generosity. No, It is flowing forth in the same way as the earth gives forth vegetables, fruits, and flowers. Out of its goodness? No! Out of the abundance of the life and love of the Father which pours Itself through, and out into, all creation.

In seeking your good outside yourself, you are living in a world of division because to your sense of things there is just so much good manifested on earth, and there are three and a half billion people on earth asking for some of it. Therefore, the moment you divide that which is already visible and use it up, you are leaving nothing but depletion, lack, and limitation behind. Even if there were enough to go around, that would be the end of it the moment it is divided.

The person following the spiritual way of life never thinks of drawing his good from that which is already manifested out here. In other words, he does not live or depend on yesterday's

---

[7] Hebrews 13:5.   [8] Ruth 1:16.

manna: he lives as if God were flowing forth twenty-four hours a day forever. So the Christ-life is one of looking within and realizing that you are not seeking to divide what is already out in the world, but rather to multiply the loaves and fishes now established within your own consciousness. Whether you are thinking in terms of potatoes, dollar bills, friends, service, devotion, good, or healing, it is not what is already in the manifest world that you are seeking, but the continuous flow from the Father within, the multiplication of loaves and fishes from within.

Do you know that each one of us could have all there is on earth, and still everyone else could also have all there is on earth? Do you know why? Because this is a spiritual universe. Every potato in the soil is spiritual, and it multiplies itself, end without end, unless you stop the flow by trying to divide it, get it, or bring it to you, instead of opening a way and letting it flow into expression. How do you do that? Close your eyes, turn within, and realize:

Father, within me is the infinite, the limitless, spiritual universe. Let it flow. Let me be the avenue of healing the multitudes, feeding the multitudes, of understanding, helping, companioning, and aiding them. But let all this flow as a service unto Thee.

When you do this, you will find what it means to live in spiritual companionship, and you will know the meaning of "the tabernacle of God is with men." [9] The tabernacle, the temple, the beauty, the allness, the harmony, the grace, and the peace are here and now, but only as you withdraw your attention from

● Revelation 21:3.

that which is already manifest in the world and give up trying to divide it.

You cannot live in the Fourth Dimension and draw from the outer realm, because the Fourth Dimension is the source of that which is in the outer realm, and you bring it forth for the use of those who do not yet know how to draw on the infinity of their own being.

Suppose that you should awaken and find that the Christ is your real being. Would you not then feel foolish to seek supply? Would you not rather realize that you could feed the whole community, and have a surplus left over? Is not the Christ your life, your being? Is not the Christ the only law unto you? Is not the Christ your sufficiency, the only quality and the only quantity? How, then, can you live as the Christ and look to "man, whose breath is in his nostrils" [10] to divide what he already has?

Turn within! Be assured of this: the Master made no mistake when he revealed that "the kingdom of God is within you." [11] The kingdom of Allness is within you, and if you wish allness and an abundance of allness, then turn to the kingdom of God within, and stop this looking to "man, whose breath is in his nostrils."

[10] Isaiah 2:22.
[11] Luke 17:21.

"Awake Thou That Sleepest"

————◄●►————

The New Dimension is the revelation of a Presence and Power that cannot be defined by human thought, and which ordinarily is not brought into play in human experience except by those who have caught the vision of a spiritual universe.

The thinking of the average human being does not penetrate the realm of the Spirit. His entire life, his reasoning faculties, and his awareness remain in a three-dimensional world, a world that can be thought about and known only from the standpoint of the physical senses. In that realm, all forms of human power —might, strength, wisdom, and cunning—are either aiding or harming us, being used either constructively or destructively. The entire human world is made up of pictures, sometimes good and sometimes bad, and of the reactions that come to a person from what he beholds with his five physical senses and with the reasoning mind.

The few who penetrate the veil and see into the spiritual Real discover that there is another Power and Presence that is neither power nor presence in the human sense of understanding. To material sense, It is not presence because It is not outlined form; It is not power because It does not supplant, overcome, rule, or govern other powers. Yet, It is a presence in the sense that the spiritually illumined feel It, sense It, cognize It, and are aware of It, even while It has no actual form, outline, color, or dimension. It is a power because Its very presence reveals harmony, even where discord, disease, or sin may have been.

The mystics of all ages—and the word "mystic" means, of course, anyone who has attained some measure of conscious oneness with God—have discerned this invisible Presence and Power and availed themselves of It; and through It, they have risen to great heights of peace, harmony, and joy within their own being.

Although many of these mystics suffered persecution from the outside world, this never disturbed their inner being because they understood the reason for this persecution. They realized that this Power would destroy those, and the activity of those, who might permit its entrance into their consciousness and who were not yet ready to see the advantage of giving up their personal sense of life for the divine or spiritual life. For the materialist, it is very difficult to imagine being happy or being wealthy by giving, when all his training has been that happiness and wealth are to be achieved by getting and possessing.

This three-dimensional world, which is called the human or material world, really is only a false concept of the Real and is never destroyed, in and of itself. *It is seen through!* It is understood for what it is, and in that understanding comes the dissolution of it. In other words, there is in reality no such thing as an objectified, physical, mortal, material universe. The only universe that exists is the spiritual real world of God's creating, and the proof of this is that the moment a degree of inner vision is awakened the world of God's creating becomes the only real world, and the mortal concept begins to lose reality and to disappear.

As long as there has been recorded history, there have been secret religious orders or brotherhoods, formed for many different purposes, under many different names, and all requiring some form of initiation. The initiates must undergo certain trials, tests, and examinations before they are admitted to brotherhood; and while the actual initiation may differ in its exterior form, the tests and trials and examinations are all alike in this respect: the initiates must go through difficult and terrifying experiences.

For example, in their meditations and in their periods of quiet, they behold pictures of their loved ones dying, being killed, or robbed. They may even see visions of betrayal, falseness, or deceit. The temptation, then, is to leave the order and quickly return home to protect their loved ones, or to do whatever is necessary to restore harmony in their experience. At each one of these steps, some initiates do succumb to these temptations and go home, and that ends their spiritual progress. Others find themselves in harrowing experiences of a different nature and they, too, drop by the wayside.

Eventually those who survive the simpler tests and temptations come to the ultimate one. The final test is that of being faced with death in some form, such as being brought to the brink of a cliff, and being told—and of course one must be obedient—to jump off the cliff onto the rocks or the waters beneath.

The cliff is so high and the rocks below are so jagged that there is no hope of survival. To jump means death. Which will it be: death or disobedience? If it is disobedience, there is no hope of being admitted to the Brotherhood. If it is death, that also ends all hope. But there are some brothers in the order; and therefore some must have survived the test; some must have endured and come through the ordeal.

There is the test, a test which each one within himself must decide to take or not. Needless to say, anyone who is obedient and jumps off the cliff automatically becomes a member of the Brotherhood because long before he can reach the rocks, he has awakened and found that the whole experience was an illusion. He had been hypnotized into seeing and accepting all these pictures, but from the very first to the last, none of them was ever real.

And what about those whose fears prevented them from stepping out into the unknown? They went home, found to their dismay that none of the things they had feared had ever happened, and they had lost their chance for spiritual progress.

Those who survived the final test were admitted to the Brotherhood, but something far greater had happened to them than becoming a part of a spiritual order. They had learned the great secret that all human experience is a state of illusion, and that the conditions they had been tempted to see and believe did not exist anywhere in the realm of the Real.

Today we are the initiates, and right now we are taking the degrees of brotherhood. Right now, we are being tested and tried with experiences of lack and limitation, sin, or disease. We may not realize that we are undergoing an initiation, but we are. Some of us are even being tested by the appearance of death, but what a revelation it is to see the look on the faces of some of the people who thought they had died! They are surprised when they awaken and find that the whole experience is illusion, that it never happened, and that they are beginning right where they left off.

The human mind cannot pierce the veil of material sense any more than the initiates in the Brotherhood could see through the temptations presented to them while under hypnotism. It is only as they come out from the hypnotism that some, by divine Grace, receive enough light to know that they had been hypnotized and are thus enabled to disregard the experiences they have gone through. Others, still under a measure of hypnotism, believe that what they are experiencing is real and run out to *do* something about it.

Everyone who has been responsible for spiritual healing knows that he has never healed a disease or set a bone. All he has done is pierce the illusion of hypnotic suggestion and see through to the world and the man of God's creating, see that God is the only life, the only wisdom, the only law, the only substance, the only cause, and therefore the only effect.

The faculty that enables one to pierce the veil, to see through the illusion, is the Christ. It is spiritual consciousness, and spiritual consciousness means the consciousness of the Spirit. Quite obviously, material sense could never have that faculty.

Some, fortunate indeed, come into this plane of existence with a measure of that illumined consciousness—enough, at least, to behold some degree of Reality. Others, and most of us are in that category, see only the mortal, material sense of things, and find it very, very difficult to believe that there is a universe of harmony here and now, and that we may enter it at will—not by choice, but because there is no other universe. All that is necessary to behold it is a tiny measure of that touch, that Christ-consciousness.

So the question comes to us: How do we attain the ability to see through the illusion and to know that it is safe for us to "jump," since the only place we can "jump" is into the Everlasting Arms? The answer is that you already have the first seed of that illumination. It is because you had that seed that, in the beginning, you set out on a spiritual path. It was that spiritual seed that drove you there. Unless you had had it, you would not have come to any spiritual teaching. It would have bored you; it would have angered you; it would have seemed nonsensical to you because "the natural man receiveth not the things of the Spirit of God: for they are foolishness unto him." [1] The mere fact that this is not foolishness to you is an indication that you have already risen above the level of mortal man.

You have no choice but to continue, nor need you have any doubts or fears about the ultimate result. The fact that you have been placed on the Path is enough. Probably the fears or doubts you entertain about your ability to attain may, for a while, prevent your attainment, but the greater your ability to relax and to understand that you are not on this Path of your own choice or by your will, but that a seed was planted in you and that it is sprouting—the more you can realize that, and just step aside and let it take its normal course—the more quickly will you awaken into your membership in the Brotherhood, into the realization of spiritual being. It is inevitable! You cannot miss!

The awakening is an act of Grace. It is an act of God for which you have no personal responsibility. The government is upon His shoulders. Only mark this: As you look out on this world from the standpoint of appearances, you will see yourself struggling and striving to achieve spirituality, and the longer you look at life from that standpoint, the greater the struggle. But in this very moment as you drop that barrier, as you drop the sense

[1] I Corinthians 2:14.

of looking out at a world of illusion and trying to improve it, you can sit back quietly in the realization, "Certainly! Certainly! What else is true? What else is logical than that God is the creator of this universe, and if the creator, also its maintainer and sustainer? If this is true, and we are living in a state of illusion, what could be truer than that only God could be the destroyer of the illusion?"

Where, then, is your personal responsibility? It is to be normal, be natural; it is to live every day in accordance with the pattern that is placed before you in the morning. Keep in thought, insofar as is possible, that you must never judge either man or circumstance from the standpoint of its appearance. Stop looking at sick and sinful man and wondering how to make him well. Stop looking at the pictures that are painted in the newspapers, on the radio and television, and stop wondering how you can improve them. You are not going to improve them: illumination is going to dissolve them, and the greatest part of that illumination is the realization that only God can do that.

The world may not see it or be aware of it, but the fact is that the redemption of the world through the revelation of its spiritual perfection and purity is not only inevitable, but it is not even far-off. Progress toward that end is so rapid that I would not be surprised if I woke up tomorrow morning and found the entire world at peace and in the arms of God.

It is only three or four hundred years ago that there was no Scripture in circulation. It is only five hundred years ago that a printing press printed the first copy of the Bible, and even a hundred years later there were not many copies in existence, that is, not many for the layman. So it has only been in the last few hundred years that men and women have had access to Scripture, which is a revelation of the power of love and of the power of Grace, a revelation of God in individual affairs.

It is only in these last hundred and fifty years that the great art, music, and sculpture of the world have been made available to the common man. Education, up to that time, was primarily for those who entered the church, but for those outside the church there was very little such opportunity. So all this cultural, philosophical, and spiritual good has come into widespread awareness in just these last few hundred years. Furthermore, it is only in the last seventy-five years that the world has had the revelation of the true nature of what it is facing as human experience. Up to that time, the world was battling evil as if it were a reality. It was battling the devil as hard as if it were a four-alarm fire, and not making much headway with it, either.

In this last three-quarters of a century, the world has become less afraid of hell and damnation, less afraid of God, and less afraid of disease. In other words, human consciousness is rapidly becoming illumined with the understanding of the grace of God, illumined with the understanding of a divine Presence and Power, and above all, illumined with the forces of love. You can see how love is being expressed in tangible form in improved business relationships in the country, in the greater efforts of nations to help other nations and of peoples to help other peoples. In spite of the prejudices and hates that still continue here and there, the over-all scene has greatly improved.

When human consciousness is filled with a sense of love and peace, a sense of an all-abiding and all-powerful Presence, it is not far from heaven, from spiritual realization. That is now happening, and happening very rapidly. If you were to judge the world from the standpoint of appearances—its many wars and the nations in distress—the change that has taken place might not be so evident to you. But look at it from my side of the curtain, and you will see not so much the outer struggle and strife that is going on, but the astonishing degree of illumination that is entering human consciousness. That is the picture I am seeing.

Let me carry this a step further even than that. If we are to be a light for the rest of the world, we must not become fascinated or hypnotized by the world of appearances, but even with this little understanding that we have been given, and have to this moment demonstrated, we must see beyond the appearance world and look at it always from God's side. That ultimately is going to be the saving grace: the ability to look out into the world from God's side, not from the side of appearances.

Herein lies the secret of dehypnotization, that is, the secret of waking out of the illusions of sense: temptation, mortality, ignorance, and superstition. Look out from God's side. First of all, be sure in your mind that you have caught a glimpse of God as the infinite power of good, as the infinite substance and law of the universe. Then, as you look out from God's side of the world, you will find a God-governed world, a God-maintained and a God-sustained world; and whatever the illusion appears to be, you will find God to be the destroyer of it. As you realize this, personal responsibility drops away, and you know that you do not have to struggle for enlightenment. It is coming to you as fast as you can accept and respond to it.

Just continue in the path in which you find yourself; continue in the way that will satisfy your own integrity that you are doing all that can be expected of you, that you are living up to your highest sense of right. Beyond that you have no responsibility. The government is on His shoulders.

Looking out at this world from the God-side, you witness a degree of individuality, based completely on spiritual values that show you that man does not have to be saved or healed. What man does need, however, is to awaken. But since one with God is a majority, when one awakens—and that means one Christ— that one can awaken millions, millions, and millions! One Jesus, rightly understood, can awaken millions of people on the face of the earth. It takes only one, one who has the light that sees behind the human scene to the spiritual scene.

There is no solution to the human scene through human means. There is no solution to the human scene except waking up out of it. Whether it is the unsatisfactory relationship that has existed for many years between capital and labor, or whether it is the unhappy relationship between two persons, there is no human solution to it.

Let one person believe for a moment that he derives his good from another, let him believe that his interests are antagonistic to another's, and you have the ingredients for all the wars, discords, ulcers, and all the troubles that ever could be in a universe of millions of people. Just multiply the human relationship existing between almost any two persons, and then you will find of what the human world consists, and you will also know that there is no solution to these cleavages on the human plane because always one will be seeing what his rights are, and the other will be seeing *his* rights. One will be seeing his privileges, and the other will be seeing the other's duties, and so there is no coming together.

The solution lies in spiritual means. As you begin to see that "man, whose breath is in his nostrils" is not a reality or an evil but an illusion, and that actually there stands the Christ, as you begin to understand the spiritual nature of individual being, you will begin to see a change in relationships, even if in the beginning it is only on the side of the one who has caught the first glimpse of spiritual light. Then you will find less antagonism, less greed, less anger, less fault-finding, and less of the negative qualities of humanhood.

It would be an utter impossibility for one individual to live consistently in a consciousness of love and forgiveness and not have the other eventually respond in some measure—or be re-moved and leave room for someone else to come in, in harmony, in peace, with the New Dimension, the Christ.

When you see this universe from the standpoint of Christ as individual being, when you look through the appearance to the reality, letting every opinion, thought, and conviction stem from God, then the world will begin to come to you in this New Dimension, perhaps not entirely because there still is plenty of hardened thought in the world, but that is not your concern. Your concern is that you begin, and since you and I are of the household of God, and we have caught a glimpse, at least, of true Being, we are the ones who must do this in our own way.

The truth is that we have no choice in the matter. We are the ones who must do it, and we are the ones who must continue to do it because of the measure of Grace that has been given to us, the Grace to know that God is the principle of this universe, that love is the real influence on earth as it is in heaven.

So, because we know these things, and because knowing them, we cannot unknow them, it becomes natural for every one of us, to some extent, to obey the impulse to behold spiritually rather than materially. Because of that and because of the fact that this will continue to grow upon us, it is inevitable that this light will go further and further into human consciousness until all human consciousness is illumined.

Our greatest concern must be a concern for our individual responsibility: Can I do enough? Will I do enough? Will I meas-ure up? That is why I would like to say to you that you will not measure up, but neither will you fail. Neither success nor fail-ure rests upon your efforts: you are but the instrument through which the Christ is finding entrance into human consciousness. That is what you are! I say "you," but you know I mean "we." That is what we are! We are the instruments now being used by the divine Consciousness to spread Its light into darkened consciousness, into the consciousness of what is called "this world."

The responsibility is not on our shoulders; the choice is not ours! We have no power to become like Lot's wife: we have no power to turn back, not even the power to look back. Whatever it is that we have left back there is gone. We have no choice but to continue forward. Why? Because we did not bring ourselves to this state of consciousness in the first place! "Ye have not chosen me, but I have chosen you." [2] There is something in your consciousness and mine that has prepared us to be the Light of the world: probably only a little bit of a light right now, but nevertheless, the Light of the world, and It will continue to express Itself in us and through us. It will maintain us; It will sustain us; and wherever necessary, It will destroy the illusions of sense so that we can perceive the mesmeric nature of the world looked at from the standpoint of appearances.

No one who has worked with the principles of The Infinite Way for any length of time will ever again be quite as hypnotized by appearances as he was before. Nobody ever again can be quite as horrified by the bad pictures, nor can he rejoice quite as much in the good pictures, since everyone who has dedicated himself to this work has been touched by the Christ to the degree that the appearance world will never again be quite as disastrous or fearful.

Once we have beheld the very presence of the Christ or experienced Its activity, how can that leave us untouched, or how can that leave us where it found us? We might doubt our own ability to understand or progress, but can we doubt the ability of the Christ to perform Its functions in us? Is the Christ ever-present to no avail? Does the Word return void? No, not when you are

2 John 15:16.

talking about deific power, Christ-power, the presence of the Spirit Itself!

There is no such thing as a touch of that Finger, there is no such thing as a grain of illumination that does not appear in the outer world as greater harmony, greater peace, greater health, greater supply, greater joy, greater something-or-other of a spiritually good nature. Impossible! So, even were you to doubt your own capacity, even if you were to doubt your own motive in studying this message, do not doubt the activity, the presence, and the power of the Christ once you have felt It, been touched by It, or have seen It. Never!

But if you should doubt It, go ahead and doubt because even that will not interfere with the ability of the presence and the power of the Christ to destroy every illusion of sense. Nothing that you or I might do or leave undone can ever interfere with the coming to fruition of the presence and power of God. All our faith must be placed—no, it must not be placed! Do not have any faith in It, if you cannot bring yourself to that point. What difference will your faith or lack of faith make to God or to the Christ? Can Its activity be stilled once It has been realized? No! So whether or not you and I doubt, whether or not we fear, whether or not we think that we may not live up to this, it is all the same.

The Finger has written. There is no question about that! The Handwriting is on the wall. Our consciousness has been touched. It has been touched to the extent of bringing us together all on one Path, all of one mind, desiring but one thing: more light, more light. So just being together on the Path makes us benefit from whatever light, hope, courage, or faith there is in our neighbor's consciousness. We not only benefit by the activity of the Christ, but also from the light that our neighbor has caught. This is one time when it is legitimate to borrow light from our neighbor, and not only may we borrow it, but the light from his consciousness is shining upon us, and each one is benefiting in a measure from the consciousness of every individual who has caught a glimpse of the Light.

The result is inevitable! The tiny measure of Light that we have glimpsed will pour forth into this universe in ever-growing brilliance, not only lighting us on our way, but what is more important, proving to be a light unto those who are still in darkness. Why is this? Because of you and me? No! Because the activity of the Christ is inevitable, because for hundreds of years the activity of the Christ has been penetrating human consciousness, opening it wider and wider and wider, giving it ever more light, and more light, and more light, until we have reached this glorious age when not only have we seen and felt the Light which is God, but we have caught a glimpse of the greatest truth ever revealed, and that is that the appearance world is not a world to be destroyed, but to be understood, seen through—not feared, not hated, not battled—seen through in its nothingness, in the illusory nature of its fabric.

No greater blessing will ever come to this world than the realization of the fact that we must not be fooled by appearances. And once the Light has touched us, we cannot be. Those who are fooled by appearances to the extent of deadliness, dullness, grossness, superstition, and fear are those not yet awakened or touched by even the tiniest measure of Light; but in the degree that this Light penetrates consciousness, in that degree do the illusory pictures of sin, disease, death, lack, limitation, war, volcanos, earthquakes, and all the other evils of human existence disappear from off the face of the earth, because they never had existence as reality. Their only existence was the same as the initiate's experience in the Brotherhood: it was one of hypnotism!

When those periods of temptation to believe in some particularly evil overpowering appearance come, and come they do and come they will, be alert. Remember quickly that you are not dealing with the appearance as it seems to be: you are dealing with an appearance that has no substance and no law. It cannot do any harm. In the measure of your quick response, will your freedom come from the fear, the doubt, and the delay in the realization of good.

TWELVE

"Fishers of Men"

In spiritual literature and in Scripture, there are many references which might indicate to you that you must change your way of life or you must do something in order to earn the grace of God. Remember what I say to you now: The responsibility is not on your shoulders, nor is it on any other person's shoulders. Therefore, I ask you to refrain from all indulgence in criticism or judgment of everyone in the world, and more particularly judgment, criticism, condemnation, and belittling of yourself and your own understanding because the responsibility to improve yourself is not on your shoulders: it is on the shoulders of the Christ.

Rest more in the realization of the Christ as that which is leading, guiding, and directing you. Never believe that the saints and sages and seers of the world, by some great act of their own will, became saints, sages, and seers, because it is not true. Even in this age, we have seen enough of the beloved spiritual lights—teachers, leaders, practitioners—to know that they, by their own will or grace, never gave up their personal sense of life to become spiritual teachers or leaders, but rather that the grace of God pulled them out of the business world or out of their housekeeping duties, and made of them "fishers of men."

The Master walked the hillside and as he chose each disciple, his promise was, "Follow me, and I will make you fishers of men." [1] Perhaps you think that they were men of high understanding because they obeyed. No, they had no power not to obey. They had no more power to resist the Master than you and I have right now. When the Master says, "Follow me, and I will make you fishers of men," you will obey. You have already obeyed in the sacrifice of time, money, effort, study, and meditation that you are making. You have already shown that you have no capacity to resist the activity of the Christ in your consciousness, even if you had the will or the desire, which, of course, you do not have. But if you had, and if you lacked the understanding, the wisdom, courage, or the determination, it still would make no difference because there is that in you which is greater than your human sense of rebellion or your desire for ease in matter.

Yes, the human being has a normal, natural desire to be at ease, but few human beings spend their time, effort, and money to learn more about God as you have already done. Oh, no! The human being has weddings to attend, and funerals, and jack-

[1] Matthew 4:19.

asses to raise out of the ditch. The human being has so many things to occupy him—tickets for theaters, meetings to attend, sports events—that he does not respond to the activity of the Christ. But once the Finger has touched a person, and he is called, rest assured that he will follow!

After they were chosen, did the Disciples have any responsibility for their careers? No! The Master sent them out. He sent them out without purse and without scrip, and they went the way he sent them, and they survived. He sent them out on another occasion with purse and with scrip. They went and they survived. He took some of them to the mountaintop—he took them. Did they go of themselves? No, he took them. Did they have the power to resist? No! Nor have you, nor have I. This is a life by Grace. Everything that transpires in your life today, and everything that transpires from now on unto eternity is, and will be, an act of Grace.

Oh, I know there are a few of you—maybe I am one of those few, too—who will resist that for a little while. Here and there you will turn aside to indulge some personal sense, some personal will, some personal ambition, but you will be forced back because it is not given to you to resist the Christ. It is not given to you to refute or to refuse when the call comes. True, you may be guilty of denying the Master, even three times; you may be guilty of betrayal; you may be guilty of falling asleep in your Garden of Gethsemane. What difference does it make? Do not be disturbed by it; do not be alarmed by it. Do not condemn yourself for your shortcomings. Just realize that that is part of the illusion that may be inevitable, but because of divine Grace, ultimate salvation is even more inevitable.

It is much more inevitable that Peter heal a man at the Temple Gate Beautiful than that he deny the Christ. His denial of the Christ was only an incident, one of those little instances of a human being falling temporarily by the wayside to secure popularity with the masses or because of fear of punishment. Do not judge this too harshly. You may do the same thing. You may! There are persons in this world who for some reason or other temporarily are permitting themselves to forego their full-hearted devotion to their following of the Christ. But be merciful, kind, and just to them. That is just a little tinge of humanhood. That is really not any different from Peter's denial of the Christ, not any different from the falling asleep of the Disciples in the garden. There is no real harm in it: it is but a temporary lapse.

The inevitability is that, in spite of all of those experiences, the Disciples would awaken and have the Pentecostal experience in which the Holy Ghost descended upon them, and they would hear, in their own language, the language of the Spirit, and from then on, go about their Father's business. Even then, they made the mistake of thinking that they could pool their resources and live contentedly by dividing them among the members of the group. This, however, ultimately led to the conclusion that everybody has to live by his own state of consciousness; everyone has to demonstrate his greater or lesser income; everyone has to demonstrate the harmonies and comforts of life: not by might, nor by power, not by dividing what is already in this world, nor living off another, but by the degree of his own demonstrated Christ.

In the fourth dimensional world, you live by Grace—"not by might, nor by power, but by my spirit." [2] Each one is responsible for his own integrity; each one is responsible for his own unfoldment; but if you judge from the world of appearances, while you are on this forty-year journey through the wilderness, you may

[2] Zechariah 4:6.

well find that there is some slipping, slipping backward quite a long distance, too. You may be surprised and shocked at some of the things that you see even in those who apparently have gone some distance on the Path. But be charitable. Remember that that is just a little human weakness, and you may be sure that the Christ is going to dissolve it because the activity of the Christ is the dissolution of humanhood, of your weaknesses and your illusions.

Patience! Patience! You have an eternity in which to work out your salvation. Patience! Be patient with one another, and be patient with yourself. Forgive yourself, and as often as you fall down, pick yourself up again. You have no choice! Inevitably, the Voice will sound in your ear, "Come! Follow me, and I will make you fishers of men."

You will know then that it is *I* calling. You will know then that it is not your will, and therefore, you cannot experience either success or failure. Remember that you cannot succeed or fail. Why? Because *I* have called you and made you "fishers of men," and it will be *My* success working in you and through you for *My* purpose, and you will be but the instrument.

In moments of temporary or seeming failure, please remember that that, too, is part of the plan, and probably part of the plan to teach you that you cannot fail and you cannot succeed because the *I* that called you is the only success.

"Follow me, and I will make you fishers of men." *I* will do that. What is this *I*? Who is this *I*? Where is this *I*? Is not this *I* of our being God? Then, which is more potent, a material remedy or *I*? The dollars in the bank or *I*? "Follow me, and I will make you fishers of men." Follow the *I* within you, the Father within.

Follow this Christ, this Principle, this Spirit that abides within your own being, and see if in relinquishing your material dependencies in life a higher, finer, more joyous spiritual life as manifested in better health and more abundant supply does not unfold.

Can you leave all your material dependencies? Can you leave your dependency on your family for love, justice, and mercy, and expect these only from the Father? Can you turn from expecting justice from a judge and jury, and expect it from the Father within your own being? Can you turn from expecting gratitude, reward, recognition, or appreciation from your employer or employees, or from members of your family, and seek your good only in the Father within you? Can you follow only the Spirit within and not the personal sense without?

Where are you now in consciousness? Are you still at that place where you say to the Master, "No, go on for a season, I must catch more fish for my family. Go on, while I stay behind here and rely on human beings for recognition and reward, and for cooperation and gratitude." Or have you reached that point of consciousness that the Disciples had reached when without question they laid down their nets?

The Master was not asking those men to follow a man named Jesus. He was asking them to follow the teaching that the *I* within is the Messiah. And today no one is asking you or your students to follow a man or to follow a book, but to follow *Me,* the *I,* the Spirit, at the center of your being. Leave your "nets" and follow the *I.* Leave your material modes and means and follow the *I,* the Spirit within you, the divine Christ, and trust It rather than trust something or somebody out here in this external realm.

Some of you, at least, have reached a point in your spiritual development where you are being called upon to choose this day

whom you will serve. Some of you have not yet left your "nets."
Some of you have not yet left your reliance on and confidence
in material means and in human beings. Some of you have not
yet learned to rely completely on the Father within. But now
you are being called upon to leave your "nets."

THIRTEEN

The Inner Vision

————◂●▸————

You have come to that point in consciousness where you are seeking for what the world calls the intangible. When you came to a spiritual teaching, you knew in advance, or soon learned, that you were going to obtain nothing in the external realm. What you were seeking was the Invisible, that which cannot be seen, heard, or known. And yet you were seeking to be able to see, hear, and know just that. Through that seeking, you are coming to know that which is unknowable, see that which is invisible, hear that which is inaudible. And on this Nothing you now live.

He "hangeth the earth upon nothing" [1]—nothing that you

[1] Job 26:7.

will ever see, hear, taste, touch, or smell. But of this, I am sure, if you are persistent and faithful, the day will come when you will feel It, see It, hear It, and know It, even though there is no *It* to see, hear, feel, and know.

What was it that separated the followers of the Master from all other Hebrews? Only that those who were not Jesus' followers could not see, hear, taste, touch, or smell what it was that the Disciples and the Hebrew Christians had accepted as the truth. It was foolishness to them, nothing but foolishness! How can anyone follow something that nobody knows anything about? And then these followers of the Master would smile, "Not know anything about it? We know all about it!"

"Well, what is it? Where is it? Let me see it. Let me touch it."

"No, it is a glint in the eye."

"Ah, now! That is foolishness! That is foolishness!"

And yet, that was the truth. These people saw something in the Master; they felt something in their association with him that satisfied, so that they, too, could say, "Ah, we do not live by bread alone. We are receiving an inner Grace, an inner meat, wine, and water." They knew what the Master meant when he told them, "Take, eat; this is my body." [2] They knew what the others could never understand.

It has been said that when a person of spiritual vision went into the darkened room where stood the Cup from which the Master had drunk, he saw a light all around the rim of the Cup, but those who were not followers of the Master and who had not become Christians saw nothing but an ordinary drinking cup; and they wondered why so much ado was being made about it, and why so many people were willing to die for it.

When the Master walked the earth after the Crucifixion, it

[2] Matthew 26:26.

is said that only a few more than five hundred people ³ out of all the thousands who walked those roads saw him. Think of that! Out of the thousands in Jerusalem, only five hundred saw him! Those five hundred saw what is invisible and intangible to human sense. They saw what human beings can never see.

We, today, who have touched even the hem of the Master's robe require nothing that the world can see, hear, taste, touch, or smell. In a world threatened with atomic bombs, those of us who have tasted one drop of spiritual life, love, and truth are not out looking for bomb shelters or for cabins in some remote place. And why? Because we feel an invisible security, an invisible safety, which is that impregnable safety and security that can be found only in God.

Self-complete in God, we walk the earth enveloped in an eternal bombproof shelter. We dwell "in the secret place of the most High." ⁴ Is there such a place? Is it a place at all? Or is it the consciousness of God's presence? Is it not true that none of the evils of this world shall come nigh the dwelling place of those who live in the awareness of God's presence? That awareness is more powerful than lions and adders, than all the ills of human experience. That awareness is greater than all the evils of the world.

Any spiritual teaching is a revelation that a state of spiritual awareness, God-consciousness, is greater protection than a bomb shelter. An awareness of God's presence is a greater remedial agency than medicine, manipulations, or surgery. It is strange, but it is true.

At this period of our experience, we are being told to leave our "nets." Think of it! We are told to leave our material means of making a living, and follow what? Follow *Me*! In other words,

³ I Corinthians 15:6.   ⁴ Psalm 91:1.

we must let *I* be our food, our protection, and our healing agency.

"If ye have faith as a grain of mustard seed, ye shall say unto this mountain, Remove hence to yonder place; and it shall remove; and nothing shall be impossible unto you." [5] Yes, the whole mountain would disappear: not only a fever, not only a cold, not just a little lump: the whole mountain would disappear. How? By faith in *Me,* faith in the Invisible, in the Intangible, in That which you can never know by means of the external senses.

Every move that the Master made throughout his three-year ministry is a lesson in complete reliance on That of which the world knows nothing. Do you remember that one of the three temptations set before him was to turn the stones into bread? And what was his answer? "It is written, Man shall not live by bread alone, but by every word that proceedeth out of the mouth of God." [6]

Throughout his entire ministry, he lived in his Self-completeness in God. When the Disciples wanted to get him something to eat, his answer was, "I have meat to eat that ye know not of." [7] And to the woman at the well, he promised living water. From where? He had no bucket to draw it with, but he did not need a bucket because the water he was talking about was invisible: no one could see it, hear it, taste it, touch it, or smell it.

How does anyone know these things exist? How can anyone have confidence in such intangibles? Ah, there comes the secret! There comes the division! If you cannot feel an inner rightness about this message, if you cannot feel an inner confidence in a "medicine" that you will never see, hear, taste, touch, or smell, if you cannot have a complete faith and confidence in *Me,* in the *I* within your being, if you cannot rely on *I,* if you cannot come

[5] Matthew 17:20.   [6] Matthew 4:4.   [7] John 4:32.

to a place where you believe that "*I* am come" that you might be fulfilled physically, mentally, morally, and financially, then the thing to do is to leave this work for a season. Go back to the world of material sense until a greater degree of awareness comes, because if you seesaw between the two you will only tear yourself to pieces.

A double-minded man cannot get anywhere, and only brings confusion upon himself. Decide within yourself that you are either going to feel the love and confidence in a divine Power within you and be willing with faith to prove it and see it come through into expression, or that you are going to leave it for a season and go back to it again at another time when something arises in your life to renew or bring about a resurgence of that faith.

That is the answer to the whole of the spiritual life. It is really up to you. It is true that the Master walked up and down the shores of Galilee, but he did not proselyte. Surely he did not make speeches trying to persuade or force anybody into believing in him. As far as the records show, he walked the Holy Land, he sat in the mountains and talked with the multitudes that gathered there. I do not believe he sent for them. He just talked to those who gathered there; and I am sure that among those multitudes there must have been some who came to ridicule, to doubt, and some, like Nicodemus, who were unable to grasp the vision. There are undoubtedly millions of Nicodemuses in the world; and for them, this work has no appeal. This work has an appeal only for those who are able to respond with some measure of love, trust, and confidence.

The question now arises as to whether this message registers sufficiently within your own being for you to say, "The Christ must be my sole reliance." At one point or another, you must leave your "nets"; you must give up every material approach to life and see life from a spiritual standpoint, and then as your faith in the Infinite Invisible grows, you come to understand that He that is within you is greater than he that is in the world, and that He performs that which is given you to do.

So you turn, not because somebody tells you to have faith but because of an inner conviction. Nobody can give you faith. That is something that springs up within you, and when it does, you know that your faith is not in the visible realm, not in the *I* of your teacher or the *I* of your leader, but in the *I* of your own being.

You begin to understand the meaning of a reliance on a completely invisible Thing, so invisible that if the rest of the world knew what you were relying on, it would think you had lost your mind. It would! It would! It does! It does! Yes, show the world the tangibles: the dollar bills, the stocks and bonds, the real estate—that is where its faith lies, and that is common sense to most persons.

But the Hebrews who followed the Master did not have what men call common sense. It was not common sense for them to leave their fishing, to leave their nets to follow him. It was not common sense to answer, "Yes," when he asked in substance, "Do you have faith to believe that I can raise you from the dead? Do you have faith to believe that I can restore these paralyzed limbs?"

That is not common sense. That is uncommon sense. It is a divine Wisdom that lifts a person to such heights that he can say, "Yes, I have left all to follow the Invisible, the Christ, the Master within me. I have left all to follow the vision, the vision that the man in the street has never seen and never will see."

Think of the faith it took on the part of the Christians who allowed themselves to be thrown to the lions. They must have seen an immortal life beyond what they knew was to be their immediate death. Had they not had that vision, they could never have taken that kind of punishment. Think of Paul and Silas in prison, and singing. They must have seen something beyond the terrors of a prison; they must have seen something in the invisible realm that held out a greater hope and a greater promise even than freedom. Many persons have given up their freedom and their human sense of life for this vision. The Master clearly stated, "He that findeth his life shall lose it: and he that loseth his life for my sake shall find it." [8]

It may be true that to your sense of things your life and well-being are dependent on external aids or resources, but you will never find your spiritual sense of life while you are leaning on those material props. Too many persons have tried that way and failed. You cannot serve two masters. There are some, it is true, who have given the Infinite Invisible their entire faith, reliance, and confidence, and have not yet had their problems solved. There are some who have thrown their entire weight on the spiritual side of the scale, and who, for some reason, have not yet had the full measure of their release. To them, I can only say: Be patient! Be patient! Let the Christ work in you and through you to your final and complete redemption, and it will come about.

Leave your "nets"! Stop fishing for material fish and material remedies, and material ways of earning a livelihood, and follow *Me*. In the Master's teaching, one statement stands out above all others. If you wish, you can leave the others alone, but remember this: "I am come that they might have life, and that they might have it more abundantly." [9] Trust that *I* at the center of your being. Cling to that one thing or the equivalent of it: God's grace. The grace of God in you is sufficient for you. Cling stead-

[8] Matthew 10:39.   [9] John 10:10.

fastly and whole-heartedly to the truth that His grace is sufficient for you: His grace, nothing out here, just His grace. It will come. It cannot fail. It will come, and It will be in time.

You will never lose out because Spirit is the true reality of being. This material sense of existence is only a false sense, only a limited view of the great glory that is in store for you when you have caught the inner vision that can perceive the Christ where others see only Jesus, when you can perceive the Spirit where others see only matter. As you catch one little grain of that great truth and rely on it, the second will come, the third, the fourth, and the fifth. It may be a slow process, a very slow process. It was very slow with me, and it may be slow with you; but it is a very sure one, and a wonderful one when once it is achieved.

When the Master said, "Follow me, and I will make you fishers of men," he was appealing, not to common sense, but to the inner vision of the Disciples. Only those who have that inner vision can obey.

FOURTEEN

"I the Lord Have Called Thee"

Comfort ye, comfort ye my people, saith your God.

Speak ye comfortably to Jerusalem, and cry unto her, that her warfare is accomplished, that her iniquity is pardoned: for she hath received of the Lord's hand double for all her sins.

The voice of him that crieth in the wilderness, Prepare ye the way of the Lord, make straight in the desert a highway for our God.

Every valley shall be exalted, and every mountain and hill shall be made low: and the crooked shall be made straight, and the rough places plain:

And the glory of the Lord shall be revealed, and all flesh shall see it together: for the mouth of the Lord hath spoken it.

Behold, the Lord God will come with strong hand, and his arm shall rule for him: behold, his reward is with him, and his work before him.

He shall feed his flock like a shepherd: he shall gather the lambs with his arm, and carry them in his bosom, and shall gently lead those that are with young.

Isaiah 40:1–5; 10, 11

Do you see that the conviction that has to come to each one of us is that because the He, the It, the *I* of our being is the power, not one of us can fail? Do you see how there is no way for us to gain confidence or to lose fear until that moment of transition when we inwardly sense that He has that power, and because He has that power, we cannot fail? Do you see how this brings out, not only a sense of humility, it brings out the realization—not a quotation in a book, but the realization—that there is a He.

Hast thou not known? hast thou not heard, that the everlasting God, the Lord, the Creator of the ends of the earth, fainteth not, neither is weary? there is no searching of his understanding.

He giveth power to the faint; and to them that have no might he increaseth strength.

Even the youths shall faint and be weary, and the young men shall utterly fall.

Isaiah 40:28–30

Even the young, who depend on their muscles, who depend on their vitality or their youth, even they will come face to face with tribulations that will try them and cause them at times to fail.

But they that wait upon the Lord shall renew their strength; they shall mount up with wings as eagles; they shall run, and not be weary; and they shall walk, and not faint.

Isaiah 40:31

Through what? Through their completeness in God, through knowing that their strength is of God—not of themselves, not of their own understanding, their spirituality, or their power. No, no, no! There has to be that recognition of a "He"; there has to be that recognition of the Presence.

> Behold my servant, whom I uphold; mine elect, in whom my soul delighteth; I have put my spirit upon him: he shall bring forth judgment to the Gentiles.
>
> Isaiah 42:1

If we do not have that Spirit upon us, if we do not have that realization that there is an *I* empowering us, giving us voice, giving us strength, wisdom, and understanding, we are lost, and all our material props will fail us.

> He shall not cry, nor lift up, nor cause his voice to be heard in the street.
>
> A bruised reed shall he not break, and the smoking flax shall he not quench: he shall bring forth judgment unto truth.
>
> He shall not fail nor be discouraged, till he have set judgment in the earth: and the isles shall wait for his law.
>
> Thus saith God the Lord, he that created the heavens, and stretched them out; he that spread forth the earth, and that which cometh out of it; he that giveth breath unto the people upon it, and spirit to them that walk therein:
>
> I the Lord have called thee in righteousness, and will hold thine hand, and will keep thee, and give thee for a covenant of the people, for a light of the Gentiles;
>
> To open the blind eyes, to bring out the prisoners from the prison, and them that sit in darkness out of the prison house.
>
> I am the Lord: that is my name: and my glory will I not give to another, neither my praise to graven images.
>
> Isaiah 42:2–8

No power will be given to any thing or any person on earth: to material remedies or manipulations, to your thoughts or my thoughts. No power will be given to anything but to the *I*, to God Itself. God will give to you and to me what we require as we turn whole-heartedly to It in the realization of Its presence.

"I the Lord have called thee." Why do you think you are here on earth? Because the Lord, the divine Consciousness, has called Itself into expression as your individual being. It has called you to a spiritual purpose, and It will hold your hand. But your hand must be out, ready to be grasped, confident that God's hand will enfold it.

"I the Lord have called thee in righteousness, and will hold thine hand, and will keep thee." Think of the confidence it requires to understand that you will be kept throughout all time, throughout all ages, throughout all conditions of health and being. *I* will keep thee, and "give thee for a covenant of the people, for a light of the Gentiles."

In those days, the Gentiles were considered the ignorant, the pagan; the Gentiles were those who had not yet seen the light. And so *I* will give thee "for a light . . . to open the blind eyes, to bring out the prisoners from the prison, and them that sit in darkness out of the prison house." Only *I*, the Father within, can do that. Do you see that? That is where our reliance and our confidence must be placed. It is as if we were one with the Father right here, and all that the Father has is ours. Therefore, we must look only to that Father within, and let the rest of the world go by. As we do that, we find:

> The former things are come to pass, and new things do I declare: before they spring forth I tell you of them.
>
> Isaiah 42:9

> But now thus saith the Lord that created thee, O Jacob, and he that formed thee, O Israel, Fear not: for I have redeemed thee, I have called thee by thy name; thou art mine.
>
> Isaiah 43:1

Do we not fail there? Do we have an inner conviction that we belong to God, that God is in us, and through us, governing, guiding, and protecting? Do we not too often feel that we are out here in the world alone, trying to find our way back to God, instead of realizing that we have never left God, and God has never left us?

Fear not: for I have redeemed thee, I have called thee by thy name; thou art mine.

When thou passeth through the waters, I will be with thee; and through the rivers, they shall not overflow thee: when thou walkest through the fire, thou shalt not be burned; neither shall the flame kindle upon thee.

For I am the Lord thy God, the Holy One of Israel, thy Saviour. . . .

Since thou wast precious in my sight, thou hast been honourable, and I have loved thee: therefore will I give men for thee, and people for thy life.

Fear not: for I am with thee: I will bring thy seed from the east, and gather thee from the west;

I will say to the north, Give up; and to the south, Keep not back: bring my sons from far, and my daughters from the ends of the earth;

Even every one that is called by my name: for I have created him for my glory, I have formed him; yea, I have made him.

Bring forth the blind people that have eyes, and the deaf that have ears.

Let all the nations be gathered together, and let the people be assembled: who among them can declare this, and show us former things? let them bring forth their witnesses, that they may be justified: or let them hear, and say, It is truth.

Ye are my witnesses, saith the Lord, and my servant whom I have chosen: that ye may know and believe me, and understand that I am he: before me there was no God formed, neither shall there be after me.

I, even I, am the Lord; and beside me there is no saviour.

Yea, before the day was I am he: and there is none that can deliver out of my hand: I will work, and who shall let it?

Isaiah 43:1–11, 13

Gain this conviction: "I am come that they might have life, and that they might have it more abundantly." [1] *I* am come that they might have life more abundantly in every way: physically, mentally, morally, financially. "*I* am come!" Turn and gain an inner conviction that there is an *I,* a divine Presence, that not only formed you, but having formed you will never leave you, nor forsake you.

In moments of human trials and tribulations, in moments of distress, do not too quickly believe that God has forsaken you, or that you have forsaken God, but remember that even while walking through "the valley of the shadow of death," [2] the Father is right there to see you through. Even while walking through the waters or through the flames, the Father is right there; and instead of looking around for material means and material resources, look within and realize, "*I* am come that they might have life."

Only with spiritual vision, can you behold the Father. Only with spiritual intuition can you understand that there is a Christ, a divine Presence in the midst of you, and that It is greater than any circumstance or condition there is in the outer world.

Turn to that Withinness and determine to leave your "nets," to leave all and follow *Me,* the Christ, leave all, even father, mother, sister, and brother; and see if you can obey when you hear the call. Can you trust it? Can you believe it? Can you accept the fact that in the midst of you, in the center of your own being, there dwells this son of God, the Christ, your true spiritual identity, and that Its name is *I*? Its name is *I AM,* and that *I AM* is "closer . . . than breathing, and nearer than hands and feet." That *I AM* is the very law and life of your being.

This you can do only as you turn completely away from seek-

[1] John 10:10.   [2] Psalm 23:4.

ing your good from person, place, or things. Only in the degree
that you can spiritually discern the Christ as the Spirit of God
in man can you pour your love out—not draw it out, but share
what you have already beheld of the Christ with those who have
not yet beheld It.

FIFTEEN

The New Discipleship

————◄•►————

There must come a time in the experience of every seeker when he no longer tries to gain anything for himself but rather tries to help reveal this Christ that he has beheld to those now seeking It who have not yet seen It. All those who are teachers or leaders have in a measure beheld the Christ, and the only reason they have turned to teaching or to the healing ministry is to reveal that Christ to the rest of the world. That is the function of everyone on this Path.

But it is not through the human mind that the revelation comes. There must be a deeper intuition, a deeper consciousness that says to us: "I behold the Christ. I behold the Christ, even though the world tried to crucify and place It in a tomb, put a stone there, and seal that tomb. Yet I see the Christ walking the streets."

That is inner vision; that is spiritual vision; and that is the vision necessary for a complete and an utter reliance on the Christ. Nothing less will bring about healing, but when we have that, the Christ performs Its function in the consciousness of both the teacher and the student.

We cannot go out and give to the world what we have found of spiritual healing or spiritual living by talking or preaching it. The offering of the wine, the water, and the meat must be done gently and sparingly, permitting the other person to come in his own good time to his spiritual good. We cannot through preaching save the world, even though we have a principle that could and would save the world if the world could accept it.

What we can give to the world, however, is our demonstration of God. By our fruits not only will we be judged, but will we create a hunger in the world for what we have: not by offering it to others, but by letting them see how we bear witness to it.

If our faces show forth just a little bit of the glory of God, if our lives attest to the fact that we have found a principle to live by, then we may be assured that in the years to come we will reap two, four, eight, ten, twelve or more of those eager to know what it is we have found, eager to share in it, eager to be taught. That must be our gift to the world; that must be our contribution to the world.

At first it seems very selfish that we should not concern ourselves with the world, but with showing forth our understanding of the power of Grace in spiritual living. Yes, I know that sounds selfish, but we do not have too much to offer this world until we have some evidence of the fruitage of these principles. Just to offer it words and books is not offering it very much. We have to offer it understanding, and when we have enough understanding to go to others, showing forth the fruitage of a life by Grace, then one of these days the world will be eager to have it.

The greatest force, the greatest power on earth, is Grace. Grace, which is the love of God for God's children, is the only real power there is, and our demonstration of It will be in proportion to the withdrawal of our dependence on and faith in man, and the establishment within ourselves of Its power.

In other words, if at this moment I have no one upon whom to depend, no one to look to, no one to ask anything of, no one from whom to expect anything, then my good must come from the Father within, and it must come as the gift of God. Humanly I do not deserve it, and humanly I have done nothing to earn it: it must come as the grace of God, as the love of God for His own child. So, in my aloneness with God, I find myself to be the child of God, looking only to the Father within for my good: for healing, restoration, resurrection, redemption, support, maintenance, supply, success, harmony, peace, joy, protection, safety, and security—not praying for it, not asking for it, but in this quiet communion, realizing that the love of God must be all-embracing, that the love of God must be all-sufficient for the child of God; and that I have no need for any other sufficiency. His grace is sufficient for me.

As I abide in this communion with the Father, I look only to the Father within, expecting only the outflow of His love. I hold no man in condemnation or in bondage to any obligation. I forgive everybody any obligation so that whatever he shares with me is shared not because of a responsibility, a duty, or a relationship, but only through free will as a free offering of love. Therefore, I sit in my conscious union with God and recognize God as the all-embracing Love, as an All-sufficiency. Then I go about my business, performing every task, duty, and obligation in the realization that God is fulfilling Itself.

The Christ is the real Self. The Christ is that which lives our life, and rather than indulge in human suppressions and repressions, we must let life live itself normally, and whatever there is of an erroneous, material, sensual, or mortal nature will of itself disappear as we give up thinking in terms of the little "I" and think more in terms of the Christ.

In every walk of life, whether we are selling goods, marketing, housekeeping, or driving a car—whatever we are doing—as we give up the use of the word "I" and realize that it truly is the Christ that functions in us, and through us unto the world; in that degree are we giving up the self. In that degree are we "dying daily" to the sense of personal powers, personal privileges, personal rights, personal benevolences, and we are realizing ourselves as activities of the Christ.

As we do give up the personal sense of "I," we do not lack food: we have twelve baskets full left over; we do not fail in healing power: we heal the multitudes, the multitudes of those ready and receptive and responsive to the Word: not by virtue of ourselves, but by divine Grace. We have been called, and That which called us, That it is that maintains and sustains us.

In the healings brought forth by the Disciples, there was always a recognition that they were accomplished in the name of the Master, not by their own power. In doing this, they were "dying" to their personal sense of spirituality and realizing that spirituality is of the Christ, not of man. Such an acknowledgment drops the sense of personal responsibility, and makes of us a complete outlet for the activity of the Christ, putting the responsibility on Its shoulder.

This New Dimension is a dimension in which all earthly powers are proved to be no power by the Christ, by that which is neither might nor power, but which is the all-power of the Spirit. It is a relaxing of might, a relaxing of power, a relaxing of personal sense in the realization that this Invisible, and to sense Intangible, is really the only Presence and Power in our world.

That is the overcoming of the world: it is the overcoming of personal sense; it is the overcoming of vanity; it is the overcoming of the feeling of personal powers; it is the overcoming of a feeling of inadequacy. Did not the Master exemplify this in his statement, "Why callest thou me good? there is none good but one, that is, God." [1]

Do you not see, too, that the "I" announcing and proclaiming its weakness, inability, or great humility is just as much a personal sense of "I" as "I" announcing its greatness or claiming credit for something? Claim no credit, but claim no failure: *I* have called you, and *I,* the nature of that which called you, will fulfill you.

As the Disciples went forth on their mission, they were not depending on themselves: they were depending on the "He" who had called them. What they really meant was that the Power that called them into their missionary work was the Power that performed it. "The way that provides not for the wayfarer is no way to fare upon." [2]

Whatever it is that calls us out of the business world or out of the home into the spiritual ministry, that it is that accomplishes the work. By His name—by the nature of the Christ—are healings and harmonies achieved. That, however, involves giving up the use of the word "I," and the realization that the one *I* is He that calls us.

That which calls us, That it is that is interpreting the Word, enabling us to understand, receive, and respond to It, but only

[1] Matthew 19:17.
[2] Mikhail Naimy. *The Book of Mirdad* (Bombay, India: N. M. Tripathi Ltd., 1954), p. 15.

as we drop the use of the word "I" and realize, "Why, yes! He that called me is the power. It that called me, the Christ, the presence of God, the Spirit of God in man, That that called me is the power, the illumination, the guidance, the direction, the maintenance, the sustenance, the support, the all."

In the realization of this Light within us, you can see how patient we can be with our faults, weaknesses, and shortcomings, letting this Light dissolve and remove them, and reveal more and more of Its glory. This may not always come rapidly, and that is good because if it does come quickly, we may be overcome by the feeling that it was our wisdom that did it, our understanding and our spirituality, and that would be more fatal than the delay of a year, or two, or three. It is better that this realization come gradually so as not to startle us into some great belief in our own integrity or our own spirituality.

That is why this spiritual awakening is very often a slow process. It is perhaps purposely slow so that we may not be startled by too great a witnessing of miracles, and then believe that by our might or our power we have achieved these great things. To the initiate or to the beginner on the Path, that is the greatest temptation in the world. To witness miraculous healings or overflowing supply coming in and yet to be able to refrain from personal glory in the achievement is almost as difficult as for the Disciples to refrain from boasting about their power over the devils. Ah, but they had no power over devils. All that they were entitled to was gratitude that they had been called and that the Power was working through them—not that they had the power. The Power was working through them, but it could work through them only in proportion to their humility, and the true sense of humility is not any detraction or depreciation of one's self: it is a realization of one's greatness in having been called to be a servant of that Power.

Everyone who is called is a servant, not a master; and to think of oneself as a master is to lose one's place on the spiritual path because there are no masters in spiritual truth: there are only servants of the Power. That is what we are: servants of the Power. Anyone who believes himself to be otherwise forfeits whatever of Light he may have achieved!

"I can of mine own self do nothing" [3] was voiced by the one we call Master. He did not call himself Master. Master, however, is a title just as is practitioner or teacher, and if in that sense the world bestows it upon a person, there is no harm. The harm comes when a person claims to be a master. That is one of the great danger points in the way of spiritual progress, and it is a danger from which the Christ Itself in most cases protects us by making our pathway straight and narrow. If there be few who achieve it, it is for this reason: only the few can witness the great miracles of the Spirit and still realize that it is the activity of the Spirit and not of man.

In the same way, it takes a great soul to witness temporary defeat or temporary failure, and not have a sense of the personal "I" as having failed. It is difficult, but it is in those moments of temporary failure and temporary setbacks that the disciple must remember, "It is not a question of whether I succeed or fail. The Christ that operates and activates me never fails." That is the standpoint of our entire work. The Christ, the Spirit of God, is the motivating power in spiritual living and being, and It never fails. When you witness failure, you are viewing life from the three-dimensional world of appearances. Drop that, and soon you will see success coming again; but it is the success of the "He" that called you. It is the nature of the Christ to be successful and for you to be the instrument of that success.

[3] John 5:30.

From this very moment begin to accept yourself as the Vine, and from rising early in the morning to retiring late at night, remember that the Vine is the instrument through which the Father is pouring Its glory into the branches. Look out into this world, whether at people, circumstances, conditions, or governments, and see all human consciousness as the branches. Realize that, having been called as a disciple of the New Dimension, you now function as an instrument of the Infinite Invisible. Whatever your activity may be, you are functioning as the Vine, and you are looking to the Father within, the Husbandman, for continuous support, direction, love, life, and abundance—not for yourself because now you are dropping the little self. No longer will you seek good for yourself: you will seek good of the Father, only that the good may flow to the branches, to human consciousness, and by destroying the illusory sense of existence feed it, heal it, and sustain it.

Take that humblest of all attitudes, that of being the Vine. So many persons think of the Christ as something that they would like to attain because of Its greatness, not realizing that the more of It that they attain, the less they become. Never think for a moment that Jesus looked upon himself as a great man or a saviour while he walked the earth. He was a rabbi, and he looked upon himself as a servant of the most High. He was not glorified in his own time. The glorification came in the recollection of his deeds and of his humility. He was a servant, and his greatness lay in his humility, in his realization of the fact that he was a Vine and that the Father within was the essence of all that flows through the Vine to the branches.

That is why he washed the feet of the Disciples. Unless he could show them that he was but a servant, he could not prove to them that he was an instrument of God. Otherwise he would have given the impression that he of himself was some great being, and therefore, when he was gone that greatness would be gone. But he demonstrated so clearly that since he was only a servant, no matter what happened to him, the greatness would remain to flow into the hearts, the souls, the minds, and the consciousness of men in proportion to their humility.

When Peter and John raised a man at the Temple Gate Beautiful, the Hebrews marveled. "Ye men of Israel, why marvel ye at this? or why look ye so earnestly on us, as though by our own power of holiness we had made this man to walk? The God of Abraham, and of Isaac, and of Jacob, the God of our fathers, hath glorified his Son Jesus." [4] Was it not clear that they recognized themselves to be instruments of the Divine?

The great mystic Lao-tze tells us that the only way to greatness is to make oneself nothing. You can see that as a person really understands the Christ to be the allness of him, in that degree would great works come forth. Then men would give credit and glory to that servant, to that instrument, but the individual himself could receive that credit and glory only in proportion to the humility that would enable him to know that he was but the instrument for the hand of the Divine.

When you begin to perceive yourself to be the son of God, never think for a moment that you are in some way glorifying yourself. No, no, no! You are being humble and announcing your nothingness! But remember that only in the degree that you understand your nothingness can you be the servant of the most High, the instrument for the flow of God to man. In that humility and nothingness will be your greatness.

There are those who believe that we are almost insulting God to call ourselves the sons of God, or the Christ. This, we do not do lightly, nor would we ever voice it in public, but within our-

4 Acts 3:12, 13.

selves we know that the Christ is our true being and our real nature, and that as such we are the sons of God. Instead of exalting ourselves high above our fellow man, we are really submitting ourselves as servants unto him.

Only in the degree that we realize this can the term "son of God" or "the Christ" be a true name in our forehead. We enter the New Dimension, Christ, only when we enter it in the humility that knows, "I can of my own self do nothing. I am but an instrument through which infinite good is flowing into human consciousness, so that I can feed and heal the multitudes, not by virtue of myself, but by virtue of the fact that God is the life of the world, that the Husbandman is forever manifesting Itself through those individuals who know their nothingness."

Whatever our particular work in life may be, let us undertake it in the realization that we are instruments for the activity and flow of the Divine, and let It operate. Let us be sure, however, when It does, that we do not take personal credit and assume personal responsibility, and that we do not go into a decline when we go through those periods of seeming barrenness. They may not be periods of barrenness: they may be periods of rest, of further intake, like the days the Master spent away by himself doing no mighty works. When he came down from the mountain top, however, he did his mighty works, and probably we will require days, weeks, and months of refreshment in which we, too, will have the feeling of doing nothing and accomplishing nothing while the world is waiting to be redeemed. Let it wait!

"For ye have the poor always with you." [5] Do not be in too great a hurry to save them, but let them wait until the complete illumination has come to you. The only power you have to help anyone is in proportion to your being filled full, fulfilled of the

[5] Matthew 26:11.

Christ. Therefore, be not in a hurry to go out until the oil is well stocked in your lantern. Wait! Wait! Be patient!

Though the world is clamoring for healing, let it clamor. Let it wait until you are fulfilled. Then go out in the glory of the Father, in the realization of the Christ, and let It flow. When you feel the need for further refreshment, do not think that the world cannot get along without you, but rather remember that you have nothing to offer the world of yourself, and that only as you are refilled, as you become fulfilled can you go forth into the world and spread the Light, be the Christ, and show forth the glory of healing and harmony.

There was a time when it was necessary to dress up the Christ in flowing robes to attract the unthinking, but this defeated its own purpose, for the simple reason that it set the world to believing, "Ah, yes! You can do these things, but not I. Just look at that robe; just look at your background. I cannot achieve such great things."

For that reason, that type of ministry will not be successful today. Today, it is the clerk behind the counter who is the minister and the disciple, and who shows forth discipleship to the other clerks by virtue of being a clerk.

The minister and disciple of today and tomorrow will wear only a businessman's suit or a housewife's dress. There will be nothing about the minister or the disciple to set him apart from other men and women. There will be no titles and no fancy dress. The disciple cannot be glorified or set apart, nor can he function for the benefit of the world except as one of the world. Unless the world can say, "Oh, you are a man, even as I, but you can live this life; therefore there is hope for me." Only in that way can the activity of the Christ be of benefit to the world today.

No one of himself can do anything. No one of himself should feel that he is important to the world. No one of himself should feel a call to the world. Let the Christ be the call, and then when that call comes, let us be willing to retire often enough from the world to be refilled and to receive a greater awareness of the activity of the Christ.

Do we have a choice now? Is it possible for us to use this understanding for self-profit, self-glorification, or for a personal or selfish use? No! There is no choice; we have no choice. Having been called to be "fishers of men," we will have to do it in the way of the new ministry, the way of the new discipleship.

Today it is the Christ that is being glorified, not the messenger or minister of the Christ, nor the disciple of the Christ, but the Christ, the Spirit of God in man. That Spirit of God will appear in the low and the high, the up and the down, the sick and the well, the rich and the poor. Why? Because all these things are but appearances. Actually the Christ appears as the very son of God Itself, regardless of any outer mask, costume, or appearance.

We are "fishers of men," and we have been called: we have been called to witness the activity of the Christ, not to witness the glory of a man or a woman. We have been called to witness the power and the glory of the Christ and to acknowledge ourselves as instruments of that Christ within our own being, but always, to the world, to keep our fingers on the lips.

SIXTEEN

The Robe

———————◄●►———————

As an initiate, you will wear the Robe of your Degree and carry the title of Initiate, leaving behind your family name, and your family and friends as well.

Having pledged your allegiance to God and to the service of God, you have no other allegiance, obligations, or responsibilities. Having been accepted into the ministry of the Spirit, you are released from the duties and works of the earth.

In human existence, a man accepted into military service exchanges civilian clothes for a uniform, and gives up his name for a number. As a military man, he has but one obligation or duty, and that is obedience to orders.

In return for this obligation of obedience, the man who wears a uniform drops all care and responsibility for his own support. Even the support of his family comes from the military treasury. Food, clothing, housing, reading materials, amusement, vacations: all these are provided for him. The soldier takes thought for only one thing: obedience to orders. All else is given to him and provided for him. In his obedience to orders, he forsakes family and community:—mother, sister, brother, wife, and children, to obey the call and fulfill his duty of obedience.

In the spiritual life, the initiate has been called to the service and life of the Master. Immediately, he is divested of the clothing of the earthly world and given the Robe of his Degree. He renounces family ties and obligations, civil duties and activities to be of the household of God, in service to the most High.

From this moment, the initiate is relieved of all responsibility for his personal care and support. No temporal power takes over this function. Now the Infinite Invisible which has called him provides all things.

You now stand as the initiate, called to the service in the household of God, and you may look neither to man nor other temporal source for your care. Even as your spiritual meat, bread, wine, and water are supplied to you from the infinite resources of your Soul, so also the food, clothing, housing, and other human requirements are gifts of the Spirit, in which Consciousness you live and move and breathe. As your church is the temple of the living God, so the activity of your worship provides your every need.

Obedience to the call and service to the Spirit bring a deepening of consciousness, and an ever-widening understanding and spiritual capacity. The degree of your obedience, understanding, and capacity is the depth of God's unfolding consciousness, and in Its unfoldment you are lifted to higher degrees in the order of God. With the unfolding and deepening of consciousness, you will be robed in yellow, purple, and finally in white. In each Robe will be found every spiritual capacity and human fulfillment necessary to your spiritual and human support. The Robe Itself carries the responsibility of your activity and harmony and success.

Only in your Robe do you find peace, joy, contentment, activity, purity: fulfillment. Only in your Robe do you find your Self: eternality, immortality, and true being. As you were divested of your material possessions and reinvested with the Robe, so you will now find security, goodness, and satisfaction only in the Robe.

You now have no human family ties or duties: now you have only those of the household of God for companionship. As you have forsaken business or profession as a livelihood, so you will now have the Robe as your avenue or instrument of supply. You have left your forts and armies and now find peace, safety, and security in the Robe. Having left behind you every human law, you will live by this Grace, by your Robe.

Your Robe is now your abiding place: your home, your business, your pleasure, your dreams, your hope. Your Robe is your rock, your high tower, your secret place, and this Robe is your consciousness of truth.

As your consciousness of truth deepens and expands, you reach the higher degrees and planes of consciousness, each symbolized by a Robe of a different color; each demanding greater consecration, devotion, and service; and each bringing the greater rewards of silence in His peace.